HIS INSTRUMENTS

If God Could Use Them
He Can Use Us

F. Sebastian

i

HIS INSTRUMENTS

If God Could Use Them He Can Use Us

Sebastian Myladiyil, SVD

With a Foreword by
Most Reverend +Roger Paul Morin,
D.D.
Bishop of Biloxi

Printed in the United States of America

His Instruments
If God Could Use Them He Can Use Us

Copyright © 2009 by Sebastian Myladiyil

Books may be ordered through:

Sebastian Myladiyil, SVD
sebymy@hotmail.com
228-467-7347

or

Media Production Center
199 Seminary Dr.
Bay St. Louis, MS 39520

Printed in the United States of America

Dedicated to the Resilient People of the Gulf Coast, whose pain and sufferings I have shared since Hurricane Katrina ravaged the Coast

FOREWORD

This little book, HIS INSTRUMENTS: If God Could Use Them, He Can Use Us, by Reverend Sebastian Myladiyil, SVD, presents the reader with a very interesting series of meditations presenting major biblical personages from the Old Testament and the New Testament. From Adam and Eve in Genesis, to Jesus of Nazareth in the Gospels, the subjects of meditation are presented as those especially chosen humans, with the exception of Jesus Christ, whose lives are radically changed by responding to God's call for action in the world by boldly witnessing to divine love and mercy. Jesus, Son of God, the Incarnate Word, makes divine love present to all through His unique mission as Redeemer of the world.

Father Sebastian, through his thoughtful creative writing, is able to enliven individual biblical personalities as he casts them in roles of daily conversations with God as they ponder the mystery of the divine plan for them. By God's plan, each person is challenged to be faithful and loving in order to be redeemed. The mechanism and the content of the dialogical construct beckon the reader to reflect on the ways in which he or she may have talked to God about personal triumphs and tragedies, successes and failures, experienced in daily living. The inevitable discovery is that a deep personal faith forms the basis for acceptance of God's will for us. The cornerstone of unwavering faith in God's freely-given infinite love is the foundation for a blessed life that is constantly enriched by patient, consistent faithfulness.

This book of meditations is spiritual reading that will bring blessings to those who read it. I recommend Father Sebastian's mediations to those who strive for a closer relationship to God as they aspire to higher levels of perfection in the Christian life.

Most Reverend + Roger Paul Morin, D.D.
Bishop of Biloxi

November 5, 2009

Acknowledgements

Ministry in a foreign land is always challenging. God's grace and support from people are vital elements to keep the passion for ministry alive and vibrant. God's grace is ever present. I have experienced tremendous support and encouragement from many people. Tragedies and moments of crisis often bring people together. That has been my experience since Katrina hit the Gulf Coast. In coming together, I have witnessed tremendous faith, resilience and courage in many people, which in turn has deepened my own faith and strengthened my convictions.

I am so very grateful to the wonderful people of St. Rose de Lima. Words are not adequate enough to express my appreciation and love for all of you.

The members of the Society of the Divine Word have always offered support and encouragement. Thanks to Very Rev. James Pawlicki, SVD for his motivating words.

A special thank you to Most Rev. Roger Paul Morin, the Bishop of Biloxi for his enthusiastic support in this endeavor. I was elated when he agreed to write the Foreword for this book. I am grateful for his careful reading of the text and valuable suggestions.

A number of other individuals have played important roles in this effort. Ms. Chari Lee, the Secretary of St. Rose Church has diligently typed and retyped my notes. My classmate and friend Fr. Jaison Magalath, SVD, gave me valuable insight about some of the characters in the Bible. Ms. Di Fillhart's simple words of wisdom re-directed some of my thoughts about certain characters. She is the Director of SOAR: St. Rose Outreach and Recovery, formed since Katrina. Mr. Bruce Northridge has been very meticulous about proofreading and making the required corrections.

INTRODUCTION

Occasionally one may hear the questions: "Can we not leave Adam, Eve, Abraham, Jacob, Moses and all others in the Old Testament alone, and just focus on Jesus? Why bother bringing them into our lives? After all, they lived in another era. Their lives were totally different; their situations have nothing in common with us". My response is simple. We still need to consider them today, both for introspection and reassurance. They can help us face ourselves honestly and help us to be cognizant of our own mistakes, weaknesses and vulnerabilities and gain insights so we can advance in our spiritual journey. They can also give us the reassurance that just as God was present in their lives and guided them, the living God continues to be present with us and guides us.

Even though they lived in another era, and their experiences were different, they still have a story to tell us, based on their relationship with God. We would come to know their strengths and weaknesses, their dreams and aspirations, their struggles and triumphs, their victories with God or failures without God. We can marvel at the faith and resilience of some, or we can wonder about the wrong choices of others. But after reflecting upon their lives and experiences, one thing is certain: they have a lesson to teach us today that can transform us for the better. So this venture is nothing less than journeying with them, so they can give us insights as to how we can walk without faltering.

It is said, "If you see a good person imitate him or her; if you see a bad person, examine your conscience". The twenty-five persons described in these 25 sections will present before us qualities to emulate, and/or weaknesses that will lead us to an examination of our conscience. At the end of the journey when we meet the Lord, we want to be able to face Him just as we are, without any fear or shame.

We can all attest to this:

I was afraid to look at the Lord,
For I feared condemnation and judgment.
After all I deserved it
For three times I denied the Lord.

I looked within, only to find hopelessness
All that I hoped for turned to nothingness.
Denial was seen as momentary escape
Only to find it had removed my peace.

So in the restlessness of my being, I decided
To look into the eyes of my Lord.
Fearing judgment and condemnation, I looked
Only to hear him say gently "I love you more".

(Author's reflection on Peter's act of denial)

Maybe we have that fear to look up and face the Lord today. Maybe, we have that fear to face ourselves honestly. Perhaps beyond our gentle face there exists an ugly face; beyond our familiar world there exists a hidden world; beyond our loving nature there exists a hateful nature; beyond our composed demeanor there exist tempestuous personalities. Journeying with these persons in the Bible will tell us that only when we honestly face our vulnerabilities, weaknesses and limitations, can we stand before the fountains of grace, strength, holiness and perfection and hear Him say, "I love you more."

Holiness and perfection are essential attributes of God. He is holy and in Him there are no imperfections. Standing before God, who is absolutely holy and perfect, we are certainly humbled by our lack of holiness and our imperfections. Yet God invites and challenges us to move towards holiness and perfection. Leviticus 11:44 says, "For I the Lord, am your God; and you shall make and keep yourself holy, because I am holy". Jesus says in Matthew 5:48, "So be perfect, just as your heavenly Father is perfect". None of us possibly can make that claim at this time of being absolutely holy and perfect. But we can all take steps daily to come closer to this vision of God for ourselves.

Many of us are timid to take that first step because of our understanding of God or ourselves. Some say, "I am not worthy; I am not good enough; I am too weak and sinful; I have a horrible past; I am not capable; etc". When Peter encountered Jesus and witnessed the miraculous catch of the fish, his response was "Depart from me, Lord, for I am a sinful man" (Lk 5:8). Jesus was not discouraged by the words of Peter, but rather he told him "Do not be afraid; from now on you will be fishers of men" (Lk 5:10). God is not put off by our unworthiness, failures, sinful past, limitations and imperfections. He has shown repeatedly in history that, whenever men and women responded with trust and faith, they have succeeded in accomplishing His purpose.

My initial goal was to write a daily reflection for the season of Advent, based on some key figures of the Bible. Every key figure and event of the Bible somehow pointed towards the Savior, Jesus, whose coming is commemorated at Christmas. So I wanted to begin with Adam and end with Jesus - the new Adam. But as I continued this endeavor, I realized that the key figures in the Bible, both good and bad, have valuable lessons to teach us daily. We can proclaim loud and clear that "If God could work with them, He can work with us". The persons in the following chapters will tell us a lot about ourselves, maybe about our strengths and resoluteness or maybe about our sinfulness and weaknesses. Reflecting on their lives will help us both with resolving our convictions of Him and with correcting our ways, so that we can renew our strength in Him and continue our life's journey in pursuit of eternal life.

ADAM: Called for Greater Responsibility

"Lord God formed man out of the clay of the ground and blew into his nostrils the breath of life, and so man became a living being" (Gen 2:7).

There are two creation accounts in Genesis, the first book of the Bible. The focus of our reflection is the second story of creation in the second chapter of Genesis. The first narrative in Chapter 1 is a very brief, simultaneous creation of man and woman: "God created man in His image, in the divine image He created him; male and female He created them" (Gen 1: 27). The second creation story is more descriptive in the creation of human beings. It is as if God was taking His time in fashioning the crown of creation. Even the Theory of Evolution points out this time factor before the appearance of man.

God is seen here like a Master Potter using the clay and water to create His masterpiece. The mysterious anatomy of the human body required careful conception of its details along with delicate engineering skills and deliberate exercise of all powers to fashion this being into perfection. Just look at each part of the human anatomy and see how they are carefully shaped and formed for the marvelous functions they perform. God must have taken tremendous time to fashion Adam's heart and brain as these organs have both physical and spiritual functions. The faculties of these organs would enable man to reach new levels of awareness about himself, his origin, his purpose, and his destiny. Definitely it must have been such a great act of love as the Master Craftsman was engaged fully in the creation of this masterpiece.

God is not only the designer, He is also the source of life. That is the difference between God and all the other master craftsmen the world has produced. Let us consider Michelangelo sculpturing the Statue of David, chiseling away everything that was unnecessary in order to create a perfect figure. The perfect figure still remains intact for the whole world to see with that same majesty and grandeur, but without life! God, on the other hand, bends down to the newly created masterpiece and lends the greatest gift – a part of His being – LIFE so man becomes a living being!

What an act of love from God! How much joy it must have given Him when He saw Adam coming into life! Adam is not left hanging in his newly formed existence, but soon given a task that would lead him to a new level of consciousness and awareness of his being. Having created the Garden of Eden and all living creatures, God brings the creatures to Adam who has the task of naming them. God trusts Adam with this responsibility and eventually would entrust creation into his care. Adam completes the task of naming the creatures beautifully and in the process realizes a few things about himself: his superiority, his differences, and his loneliness. He realizes that he can name the creatures and that they will be known from then on by those names. He looks at all the creatures of the world and sees himself as different from them. He may also have seen the creatures in pairs and compatible therefore, but none to be suitable for him.

It is as if God recognizes this loneliness in man. God, who is a communion of persons (Father, Son and the Holy Spirit), is able to see this aspiration of man for communion, and goes to work immediately with a desire to fill this void. This is hard work, but fruitful, nonetheless, at the end. The creation of woman fulfills the deep longing of Adam for communion, as he exclaims with joy upon seeing her, "This one at last is bone of my bones and flesh of my flesh" (Gen 2:23). Here God unites man and woman to a permanent, loving and self-giving relationship.

Things should have been pretty good for the first man and woman, and indeed they were. However, Genesis Chapter 3 speaks about the fall of the first parents. The conversation between the serpent and the woman leads to an act of disobedience. Adam seems to be a silent witness to this, but a greater culprit in the act nonetheless, as it was specifically to him that God said what he could eat and what he should refrain from: "You are free to eat from any of the trees of the garden except the tree of knowledge of good and bad. From that tree you shall not eat. The moment you eat from it you are surely doomed to die" (Gen 2:16-17). There should have been moments when man and woman talked about it and felt fully satisfied with God's stipulation. Why then did he just listen to the tempting words of the serpent without asserting himself? Did the word of the serpent have such convincing power that man thought God did not tell him everything?

Adam forgot his responsibility to protect and care for the whole creation that was entrusted to him. God had made man the steward, and therefore a protector and defender of creation when "He took the man and settled him in the Garden of Eden to cultivate and care for it" (Gen 2:15). It was his duty to protect the creation from the invasion of evil. He should have defended the creation even if it cost him his life. God would never have let Adam vanish into extinction, but would have raised him up like He did with Christ, the new Adam who surrendered himself totally to the will of His Father. But Adam did not show that level of trust and confidence, and he let the evil intimidate him.

The failure of Adam consists of abandoning God's command by being a silent spectator initially, and then by disobeying Him eventually. His rebellious action brings punishment upon him at once as he seeks to hide in shame and fear. He hides like a thief, and there is no visible remorse or repentance seen in his actions, only shame and guilt. The sin of Adam leads to a breach in the harmony that existed between him and God, between him and Eve, and between him and nature. Adam lost his friendship with God and was banished from the Garden of Eden along with his wife. They also lost their access to the tree of life because God knew that having access to it would doom them to live forever in a fallen state and that was not the destiny God intended for man.

The tree of life would once again become accessible to man through the wood of the cross upon which God's beloved Son would offer the ultimate sacrifice: "And when I am lifted up from the earth I will draw everyone to myself" (Jn 12:32). Adam's sinful act had brought in death: "Through one person sin entered the world, and through sin death to all" (Rom 5:12). In contrast, Jesus would triumph over the power of evil by his death and resurrection, and restore eternal life for all. As the new Adam, Jesus would totally abandon himself to the will of the Father and in that act of surrender would bring about redemption and restoration of friendship between God and humans.

We might be quick to point out Adam's sin and blame his failure for the reality of original sin and our own fallen state. Certainly, Adam had the right knowledge and clear instructions from God as how he should live. Human tendency is to point an accusatory finger at the failure of others and justify one's own failures. In our life, we not only have the right knowledge, clear instructions, and teachings of Jesus, but we also have the example of millions who said either "yes" or "no" to God, and the results of their choices.

"Sin begins with tolerating the evil, grows with compromise, and matures in embracing it" - author

EVE: Promise of a New Beginning

"The Lord God said, 'It is not good for man to be alone. I will make a suitable partner for him" (Gen 2:18).

With bringing Eve to life, God completed creation. It may be that God saved the best for last. Seeing no suitable partner for man, God got down to the hard work. He put man into a deep sleep, almost to a state of unconsciousness, and did the first surgery. He took one rib out of man. The rib cage protects the heart and many other vital organs that preserve life. God knew the result of His creation should be dear and closer to the heart of man. Couldn't God have chosen any other bone? He certainly could have. The symbolism is great. She has to be at the side of her man – a true fitting helper, a companion in every sense of the word. In God's mind, the role of the helper, companion and spouse is to lead the other to holiness. It is the role of the spouse to protect the other from all forms of harm and to lead each other to eternal life.

Eve – Woman – as she was destined to bear children, demanded diligent and careful attention from God during the process of creation. Oh, with what tenderness and love He fashioned her! Tenderness and love then, would also become inevitable qualities of her being. God must have taken such great care in creating her because the approval also had to come from Adam. Man looked at her and fell in love with her instantly. He exclaimed, "This one at last is bone of my bones and flesh of my flesh; this one shall be called 'woman', for out of her 'man', this one has been taken" (Gen 2:23). Eve must have at once experienced compatibility in seeing Adam. Yes, they were true soulmates!

There existed perfect harmony in that original setting – between the Creator and the creation, perfect harmony within creation, and perfect harmony between man and woman, the crown of creation. Gen 2:25 says, "The man and his wife were naked, yet they felt no shame". Scripture is not talking about physical shame that comes from being naked, but points to the perfect harmony that permeated the original setting. There existed perfect love and acceptance between man and woman, and in that state of grace there was no room for shame.

The perfect unity between man and woman should have led to perfect communication between them. One of the first things Adam might have told Eve as they walked through the Garden of Eden would have been about the two trees (Gen 2:9). Eve wholeheartedly may have agreed with Adam as to how they would obey this command of God. Eve may have said that they shouldn't even set their eyes on those trees. They lacked nothing, so why go in search for anything more?

So how did the serpent get Eve's attention? Was she praised by the serpent in an unusual way? Did the cunningness of the serpent break down her defense? Whatever the case, we find Eve and the serpent in serious conversation that could be detrimental to every form of harmony. Questions are subtly posed by the serpent, and when Eve answers them the serpent gives them a twist and makes them all sound appealing without any trace of danger. The Serpent, the Father of Lies, assures her that eating the fruit will not cause them death, but would be greatly beneficial to them as they would become like gods who know the difference between good and evil. Subtly, the serpent suggests to her that God did not tell them the whole truth. The idea of being like gods must have appealed to her, for who wants to be a creature if you have the option to be the creator? Who wants to be obedient if you can be above the law?

The Serpent, the Father of Lies, seems to take advantage of the beautiful feminine qualities of tenderness, affection and the trust of Eve. By telling her "You will not die, you will be like gods", he succeeds in planting seeds of doubt in her heart. She trusted God and His word; but now she began to feel that God betrayed her trust.

One might wonder, "Where was Adam?" The horrible reality was that he was right there, like a silent spectator. Was that not the first sign of the fall? Being the "man of the house", he was exposing the love of his life to danger. This probably was the first indication of failure in his responsibility. He did not stop her from setting her eyes on the tree, touching the appealing fruit, and worse still, he silently witnessed her eat the forbidden fruit and alas ate it himself!

Shame, guilt, anger, frustration, accusatory tones and gestures all result from their failure. The perfect harmony was broken. They experienced the strange feelings of shame and guilt and they hid in fear. Love disappeared instantly and the blame game began; "it's not my fault; it's your fault." Adam wanted to put the blame on Eve, and in a subtle way blamed God for giving Eve to him. Eve, on the other hand, wanted to blame the serpent, whose words she believed!

Was Eve unjustly punished with the pain of childbearing and childbirth? Certainly for a woman these can be painful and sacrificial moments in her life. She has to sacrifice her comfort in many ways to nurture the child growing in her womb. But these could also be the most fulfilling moments of her life, when the child growing within her is the result of true love and commitment. Childbearing and childbirth can become painful moments of curse when there is lack of true commitment and total self-giving of oneself to another. When there is no total self-giving and love, what was intended as life-giving could turn out to be sinful and evil.

In pregnancy and childbirth, a woman becomes extremely vulnerable and undergoes pain and suffering. However, none of that takes away her desire to be in union with her husband. What once was presumed as part of the fullness of Adam and Eve – pure love, now has to be realized in the midst of pain and sacrifice. The pain and sacrifice are eased when there exist unconditional self-giving and love. Here 'the desire for her husband' would not lead to greater pain and suffering, but can become an expression of responsibility and pure love for one another. What appears to be a curse was, in fact, a call to greater responsibility and the promise of a new beginning.

The reality of sin had entered into human existence. There would exist ongoing struggle between the evil and the human race until the evil would be destroyed by the promised Savior. This becomes clear from God's word to the serpent: "He will crush your head, while you strike at his heel" (Gen 3:15). The new Eve, Mary, who would constantly say "yes" to God and "no" to evil would bring forth the Savior who would crush the head of the serpent. God knew that, left to themselves, human beings would not survive the struggle against evil in a fallen state. The sin was so great that no repentance or reparation on the part of human beings could restore the original state of innocence and remove guilt and shame from human experience.

The Prophet Isaiah would proclaim that the Suffering Servant – the promised Messiah – would be the one who would take away the shame and guilt: "Yet it was our infirmities that He bore, our sufferings that He endured, while we thought of Him as stricken, as one smitten by God and afflicted. But He was pierced for our offenses, crushed for our sins, upon him was the chastisement that makes us whole, by His stripes we were healed" (Isaiah 53:4-6).

In our own lives the attraction of evil can be so powerful that it can often make us forget God and His love. How often have we fallen prey to the short-term benefits and immediate gratification as a result of yielding to the tempting moments of sin? Many times short-term benefits and immediate gratification have led to greater pain and suffering in life. On the other hand, conquering the temptation of sin and attractions of the evil have led to the realization of one's true character and ultimate dependency on God's grace.

"What is right and what is wrong is already decided. It is not arbitrary. By choice we either accept or reject it." - author

CAIN: Consumed by Jealousy and Anger

"Why are you so resentful and crestfallen? If you do well, you can hold up your head; but if not, sin is a demon lurking at the door...... yet you can be his master" (Gen 4:6-7).

Life had become tougher for Adam and Eve. They had lost their privileged place in the Garden of Eden. Due to their disobedience and their attempt to become like gods, they lost their friendship with God. It was not that God had moved out of their lives but rather, they had moved away from God. While they were trying to make sense of their new form of existence, God was at work, planning for the redemption of human beings.

God had not taken away the procreative power from them. One of God's most beautiful blessings to Adam and Eve was, "Be fertile and multiply; fill the land and subdue it" (Gen 2:28). God wanted them to participate in His creative power through love and total unconditional self-giving to one another. The fall had brought in pain in childbearing. There loomed the danger of lust replacing love at any moment, momentary satisfaction replacing commitment, and self-gratification replacing unconditional self-giving for the joy of one another. The first-born in their relationship was Cain. Could he have been the result of unconditional love, lust or an "accident"? He seemed to have come to this world with a lot of baggage. The birth of his brother may have made him bitter still, when he lost the attention of his mother.

Cain might have learned the art of tilling the soil from his father. We can imagine that he was good at what he did.

Did his success make him generous? It was doubtful, as he preferred to keep the best for himself. His parents might have told him about bringing the best to God as an act of thanksgiving. But then, what may have been Cain's feelings toward God? Did he blame God for their condition? Adam might have been silent about the whole situation and Cain might not have listened to Eve when she tried to tell him about God. To make matters worse, lately she seemed to be pre-occupied with the younger son.

Cain looked down on his brother Abel, who was tending after the flocks of the family. Abel seemed to have a special relationship with God and was enthusiastic about bringing an offering from his flock. Cain did not believe in it, but still out of duty to fulfill an obligation he brought an offering to the Lord from the fruit of the soil. He looked at his brother Abel and saw him bringing the best firstlings of his flocks. He must have laughed in his heart and called his brother a fool for "wasting" such a precious creature. He might have considered himself smarter for keeping the best for himself. "Why burn up some good food for God, who lacks nothing?" he must have thought.

He was horrified at what the Lord did. God looked favorably upon the offering of Abel, but ignored Cain's. He felt totally rejected, and rage began to seep through his being. He became angry; at God, at the world, and angry at his brother. In his mind, everybody else was at fault. Then he began to see a possibility to put an end to this unhappy situation. He probably did not know that the power of sin was taking a strong hold on him as he began to forget about relationships and what the consequences of his horrible act might be. The hatred in him was so great that he did not pay any attention to the reality – the possible act of murder would deprive his parents of their children – Abel to death, and he himself, to evil.

Then he heard the gentle voice of God and His warning, "Why are you so resentful and crestfallen? If you do well, you can hold up your head; but if not, sin is a demon lurking at the door: his urge is toward you, yet you can be his master" (Gen 4:6-7). For a moment, he tried to shake off his anger and hostility. He tried to remember the many warnings he had heard about sin and its consequences. But nothing gave him peace, and he allowed the demon of sin to take control over him.

As he walked with his brother Abel to the field, he appeared calm on the outside, but fury was raging within him. He knew that he was preparing himself for the horrible act of murdering his only brother in a cold-blooded fashion. It was not an act of self-defense, nor was he trying to protect anything important to him. The violence that was raging within him resulted from allowing himself to be taken over by his passions, jealousy and hatred. The fact that his brother was innocent meant nothing to him. Cain had allowed sin and demonic power to take control over all his faculties.

He attacked his brother with such violent force that he killed him in an instant. With a triumphant heart and victorious smile he walked away when he heard the gentle voice of God again, "Where is your brother Abel?" Taken aback he thought, "no one knows about it. I did it in secret". Frustration and fury are evident in his words: "I do not know. Am I my brother's keeper?" But when he was confronted by God for the horrible act he committed, Cain realized that the consequences of his act – the murder of his innocent brother -- would hound him for the rest of his life. The feeling of victory was short-lived and it was replaced with fear and emptiness. Cain realized that he could never be at peace having killed an innocent person and depriving him of his future.

God's mercy was greater than the great sin of Cain, and He promised Cain protection even though he did not deserve it. How much suffering has been brought into human life because of uncontrolled emotions? In Cain's case it was anger, caused by his jealousy that led to his brother's murder. "You have heard that it was said to your ancestors, 'you shall not kill; and whoever kills will be liable to judgment'. But I say to you, whoever is angry with his brother will be liable to judgment" (Mt 5:21-22). Jesus was warning his listeners about the danger of this natural emotion – anger. When anger takes over a person, it leads to the 'death' of a relationship. One can cut the other person off from one's life due to the emotion of the anger. Cain had already killed the relationship due to his anger even before he actually murdered Abel.

Human passions, left uncontrolled, can bring enormous pain and unforeseen misery in life. Human beings are not called to be slaves to those passions. Every human passion can at the same time be channeled into a positive energy for the right actions in life: anger can be turned into an enthusiastic passion for justice, and jealousy can be turned into positive ambition to advance in life.

"Anger begins with folly and ends in repentance" – Anonymous

ABEL: Pure and Innocent

"Abel, for his part, brought one of the best firstlings of his flock" (Gen 4:4).

Abel, the younger son of Adam and Eve was a happy child. He loved his parents dearly, but soon became attached to his mother. Abel loved to listen to the many stories his mother told him about the Garden of Eden. The power and splendor of God continuously amazed him. He heard with sadness the story of the fall and decided never to do anything to offend God.

Abel saw remorse, shame and guilt in his mother whenever she narrated the story of the fall. Never did Eve complain that God was cruel, but she always emphasized how ungrateful and naïve she was. Neither did she blame her husband nor anyone, but constantly warned her sons about the power of evil and the need to keep away from its lies and empty promises. Cain, on the other hand, never seemed interested in listening to her stories and always walked away whenever she tried to relate her experience and warn them of evil.

Abel adored his big brother Cain. His strong, masculine figure and hard work always amazed him. He loved to go to Cain's field to eat the delicious fruits from his garden, but he was seldom allowed there. He did not complain even when Cain gave him the leftovers or spoiled fruits. He was grateful to get any attention from his brother.

As time went on, he decided to take care of the flocks of the family. He loved those lambs and took great pride in tending them. They always responded to his voice. He was sad to leave his mother and the coziness of their home and go with the flocks to the pastures. There were many dangerous wild animals searching for food. Even they seemed harmless around him. As time went on, the moments in the open fields gave him time to think of God and enjoy the beauty of creation. He was never afraid of anything, not even the wild animals, as he felt a sense of God's protection all around him. He would be lost in his thoughts of God, his heart erupting with joy at the thought of being with God forever.

When it was time to offer God the gift, he wanted to choose the best. But the best was also his favorite. There were tears in his eyes, yet joy and gratitude in his heart as he offered his favorite lamb to the Lord. He could see the gracious and loving look on God's face, and he felt his sadness lifted away and his heart experienced inexplicable joy.

He looked at his brother with a joyful smile only to find him frowning and breathing heavy. Then he noticed spoiled fruits and wasted grains as part of his brother's offering. He had seen them before, but thought nothing of it, as those were mostly what he received from his brother. Now he felt sad for Cain and asked God to accept his offering on his brother's behalf as well. He told his brother how sorry he was, but Cain walked away, apparently cursing under his breath.

It was thrilling for him to hear the words from Cain, "Let us go out in the field." "Oh, yes, I will get to see his beautiful garden. Maybe he wants me to pick the fruits and grains and help him make the offering to God", Abel thought. He wanted nothing more than God's gracious smile and favor on his brother. Then he also panicked, "could one of my lambs have escaped my attention and destroyed any part of Cain's field?" There were times when he could be lost in his thoughts as the beauty of creation reminded him of God's splendor and magnificence. There were a few sheep in his flock that could cause troubles. "Well, no", he reassured himself, "Cain would have told me if anything like that had happened".

He was greatly pleased to see the beautiful garden and its produce. The fruits were so lovely, large and looked delicious. He turned to his brother with such a great admiration and pride and told him how magnificent his garden was and how the fruits looked lovely and wonderful. He pointed to a few huge ripened fruits and suggested that those could be the best offerings for God. As he turned to face Cain, he saw the dangerous look in his eyes. It was like the cunning look of the wild animals that often came after his flocks.

He heard a thunderous roar and saw the flashing of a huge club, that came crashing down on to his skull, and he fell instantly at this heavy blow. Even in pain, he thought, "No, this is only a dream; my brother would never do such a thing". He smiled at his brother, his eyes offering him forgiveness and his heart pleading to God to be merciful upon his brother. He prayed that the blood that was gushing out from his head onto the ground would not seek vengeance, but rather would cry out to God to help his brother become a better person. Then there was another growl and a heavy blow on his head and there was absolute darkness. Then he saw a ray of light, that became brighter and brighter enveloping him totally and fully as if in a loving embrace.

The blood of the innocent Abel that cried out to the Lord was not seeking vengeance. Because, blood that seeks vengeance only multiplies violence. On the other hand, forgiveness offered in place of thirst for blood can prevent further bloodshed.

Abel stands as first in the long-line of innocent victims whose lives are taken away by the cruelty of human heart. The moment of violence that demonstrates a murderer's highest form of hate has also become the moment when the best quality of human spirit is demonstrated through love and forgiveness.

The innocent Lamb of God, Jesus, would go through the mockery of a trial and be condemned unjustly to be crucified. From the cross, Jesus would pray for his executioners, "Father, forgive them, they do not know what they do" (Lk 23:34). When the centurion who stood facing him saw how he breathed his last, he said, "Truly this man was the Son of God" (Mk 15:39). "As they were stoning Stephen, he called out, 'Lord Jesus, receive my spirit'. Then he fell to his knees and cried out in a loud voice, 'Lord do not hold this sin against them'; and when he said this, he fell asleep" (Acts 7:59-60).

Living an innocent and righteous life does not always mean one will not be exposed to the cruelties of this world. Life is often not fair, and even the most amiable can be a victim of the viciousness of evil forces. But a righteous person has the conviction that even in such situations evil can only destroy the mortal bodies, not the immortal soul and life with God.

"Whenever one can enjoy the pain and suffering of another and watch it with a sense of satisfaction, he/she has ceased to be human" – author

NOAH: Righteous Among the Wicked

"Go into the ark, you and all your household, for you alone in this age have I found to be truly just" (Gen 7:1).

Noah is introduced in the book of Genesis as a righteous person. The world at that time was in absolute turmoil and lawlessness, caused by the wickedness of human beings. God had no place in human hearts. Every conceived desire was of evil and sin multiplied in the world as a result. The evil in the world was so rampant that it made the Creator regret His decision to bring forth creation, an extension of His love. God grieved in His heart and decided to undo the creation to initiate a new beginning.

Noah stood as an exception and this was pleasing to the Lord. He was a just person and led a righteous life. "I love my Lord", he said often. Some laughed; some shook their heads; some looked aloof; some called him old fashioned; and occasionally some said he was crazy. But deep in his heart Noah knew his words were simple but true expressions of his devotion to the Lord. He was a man of faith who sought to do God's will at all times. From early on, Noah had realized the destructive effect of sin and sought the power of God to refrain from the attraction of evil. It was not easy, especially when people around him were lawless and immoral. It was a great challenge to swim against the current. There was always the tendency to go with the flow and become involved in the sinful affairs of the world. But Noah stood firm in his faith in the Lord.

Things were not pretty during his days. Noah was not the one to judge by a long shot, but human action often indicated that they either forgot about God, felt He was too distant or too busy for them, or that He was a myth and He was unconcerned about human affairs. The more people distanced themselves from God, the less human and humane they became. There was so much bloodshed, violence, shameless exploitation, and corruption. Noah felt sadness in his heart for the people, because he was convinced that if they knew the Lord, they would act differently. But there existed a bond between God and Noah that helped him to live a good and peaceful life.

Occasionally, Noah would ask the Lord, "Why is there so much corruption, so much violence, and so much lawlessness?" He could hear God say with a sigh, "They still haven't learned." One day God and Noah walked for a long time in silence. Noah was so glad to be in God's company. When he looked into God's eyes he could see compassion, sympathy, and determination. But Noah suspected the words that would come out might not be too good. Sure enough Noah heard, "They have taken my mercy and patience for granted for such a long time. It is time for a fresh start".

Noah knew when to be silent, and accepted the painful reality that God was going to destroy all mortals of the earth because of their wickedness and lawlessness. God startled Noah when He said; "You are going to build an ark, not just for you and your household, but for a pair of every living creature". He had never even imagined such a huge ark, let alone seen one. God made it clear that Noah was to save a pair of every living species as His intention was not to eliminate creation altogether, but to remake it in a new direction. Unfortunately the new direction involved destruction, the inevitable result of evil and sin.

In faith Noah began the monumental task of building the ark with the help of his sons. There was no possibility of hiring anyone for this endeavor. Now everyone began to think he was truly crazy. "Why would any sensible person build a 440 foot boat on the land?" they wondered. When the weather was great and he told them about the impending flood, they all laughed. Noah tried sincerely for years to bring others to repentance, but they mocked him. Deep within, he believed that if people turned away from their wickedness and repented, the merciful God would withhold the impending punishment. But the people ignored the warnings of Noah completely. Some even tried to stop him from building the ark, but seeing his determination they left him alone. Quite a few times he wondered if this was such a great idea. But he knew his Lord would not ask him to do anything that would be meaningless and thus lead to shame. Noah believed that God's words and promises were always true and fulfilled in time. "The Lord is entering into a Covenant with me", Noah reminded himself often.

His wife and daughters-in-law were to oversee the collection of all the food. Noah had no idea how they did it, but they got it all together for their household and for all the creatures. More surprises were in store! As he and his sons were about to complete the ark, he saw animals, wild and tame, birds and creeping creatures coming towards the ark, in pairs - male and female. Soon they were all in and the doors were closed. He knew that it was going to be the end of the world he had known and he surrendered in faith to God's plans.

The flood was no ordinary one as the waters under the earth burst forth and the waters that were gathered behind the firmament of heaven collapsed on the earth as if the floodgates of heaven were opened. For forty days and for forty nights heavy rain fell, destroying all that was evil and purifying the earth for a new beginning. Noah wondered many times if the heavy rain that fell upon the ark were God's tears. His own heart ached with pain as he could hear the loud cries for help from all around the ark and imagined the devastating destruction that was happening in the world. He had tried for years to teach the people to be obedient, just and righteous before God. However, his instruction and pleas were laughed at or totally ignored. He had to humbly admit that it was a moment of purification and that God was initiating a new creation.

The flood can be seen as a pre-figuration of baptism, a grace-filled moment through which one is purified of all evil and given a new beginning. The dove returning with an olive branch indicated to Noah that the earth was habitable. At the moment of baptism, the Holy Spirit removes the destructive power of sin and makes the person a temple of God, habitable for grace to grow and mature.

When Noah came out of the ark, his first action was to build an altar and offer a sacrifice. Pleased with it, God blessed Noah and his sons and renewed the Covenant He made with the first parents: "Be fertile and multiply and fill the earth" (Gen 9:1). The sign of the covenant would be the rainbow, as a reminder that He would never again destroy the earth due to the sinfulness of human beings.

God made it clear to Noah that He saw sin as a serious matter – one that offended Him immensely to the point of nearly bringing creation to an end. But He is a God of second chances and offered another opportunity to humanity through Noah. The question still remains, "did God know humans still would not learn?" God knew it well and understood that human hearts had become so perverse, no punishment would bring them to realize their failures. Yet God was so passionately in love with His creatures that He renewed the Covenant and made the rainbow a sign of His Covenant. The rainbow in the horizon could remind people of God's love and care. Even this Covenant would be neglected by the 'I' of human independence apart from God - the result of sin, and God's love would once again be revealed on the cross. God was setting Himself up for greater pain that involved the self-emptying and sacrifice of His only begotten Son, Jesus.

In our human nature, we often fail to learn lessons from the past and neglect the warnings for the future. We live among many who seem to think that this world is their permanent home!

"But of that day and hour no one knows, neither the angels of heaven, nor the Son, but the Father alone. For as it was in the days of Noah, so it will be at the coming of the Son of Man. In those days before the flood, they were eating and drinking, marrying and giving in marriage, up to the day that Noah entered the ark. They did not know until the flood came and carried them all away. So will it be also at the coming of the Son of Man" (Mt 24:36-39).

ABRAHAM:
Faith that Overcame all Barriers

"Abraham put his faith in the Lord, who credited it to him as an act of righteousness" (Gen 15:6).

Abraham did not hesitate to leave his father's house and land when the Lord asked him. Though he was seventy-five years old, he felt that this venture could be a new beginning. He had always experienced such a special friendship with God. He was able to talk to God like a close friend and felt safe and secure in His presence. There was a sense of peace that filled the heart of Abraham because of this love relationship.

God was always doing unexpected things in his life. He had no idea what God was up to at this time. The blessing of the Lord sounded wonderful and a little strange at the same time: wonderful, because it was the best he had heard in his life and this blessing could fulfill the greatest possible aspirations of a living being; strange, because it sounded a little unrealistic. He thought, "How could God make me a great nation when my wife and I are childless?" Never had he complained about this to the Lord, though God could see the sadness in His friend's heart. God knew what He was going to do. As Abraham listened to the blessing of the Lord, he felt strengthened by the promise and humbled at the words that echoed in his ears, "All the communities of the earth shall find blessing in you" (Gen 12:3). This at the same time became the moment of realization for Abraham that there was only One true and living God, who was the creator of the world and His love knew no boundaries.

Nothing stopped Abraham from setting forth on a journey to an unknown land. He never turned back. Twists and turns in his life continued. He had to part with his nephew Lot, and found himself in Egypt. Though Lot took the better portion of the land, Abraham moved on, trusting in God's providential care. As time went on Abraham may have wondered about the promises of the Lord. He gathered up his strength and made his frustration known, "What good will your gifts be, if I keep on being childless?" (Gen 15:2) To the delight of his ears, God answered him, "Your own issue shall be your heir" (Gen 15:4). It is so beautiful to imagine God taking his friend Abraham and showing him the sky that is lit with the numberless stars and telling him, "Your descendents shall be as numerous as the stars" (Gen 15:5).

What a promise! Optimism and freshness were returning to his life. He reassured Sarah, and trusting in God's promise they moved on. However, Sarah was getting impatient with the passing time and she probably thought God needed a little help on her part. "I am barren, but my husband must be capable, so why not give God a helping hand through my maid servant Hagar?" she thought. The impatience of Sarah only leads to greater trouble and pain for all.

God is the God of the unexpected and unimaginable things. He does the impossible, allowing Sarah to get pregnant at her old age and thereby making His promises come true. Jesus, reasserting the abilities of God, would state that, "All things are possible for God" (Mt 19:26). Isaac, the love of their lives, is born. Looking at this tiny boy, Abraham may have thought proudly, "all the promises of the Lord will come through this little child".

The greatest test of his life was yet to come. Abraham delighted in hearing the voice of the Lord. As usual he was ready to hear the loving words of God and obey them. As he listened to the words, he must have stood still for a moment thinking that it was a just a dream, and a bad one indeed! Reality soon set in on him that he was going to lose the love of his life, his only son, to the One he loved above all things. No further words were spoken. He did not speak a single word to his wife that night. Time must have stood still as he looked at the sleeping face of his little child.

He must have dreaded the moment when dawn set in. The three-day journey must have felt longer than all his previous journeys. But with every step they took, it was like closing in on the end of his hopes and dreams. He must have looked several times at his cheerful son, who was so happy to be with his father on this long journey, and more excited about worshiping God, who was everything to them. Tears may have blinded Abraham often when he thought of the final moment. Repeatedly, he must have reassured himself that God knew what He was doing and that His plans were always for his wellbeing.

He must have been crestfallen when he saw the land of Moriah. Asking the servants to remain there, Abraham and Isaac continued their journey. He might have thought with sadness about his lone return trip. What would he say to Sarah? Would she die of grief, or worse, curse God for this cruelty? Then he heard the sweet sound of his baby boy, "Father, here are the fire and the wood, but where is the sheep for the holocaust?" He must have choked when he said, "Son, God will provide".

Helplessness must have filled his heart when he thought, "God wants you to be the victim".

It must have been a painful experience to build the altar this time. He remembered the tremendous feelings of joy, awe and unworthiness he felt whenever he had built an altar previously. There was no turning back. Resolved to obey God and trust in His promises, he completed the task and tied his son and placed him on the altar. With trembling hands he must have reached for the knife. His eyes must have caught the eyes of his son and locked in for what seemed like an eternity. What thoughts of God went through the mind of Isaac as he laid still, helplessly bound and waiting for the knife to pass through his body? Though Isaac had heard of human sacrifices demanded by other gods in surrounding cultures, never did he imagine it as part of the living God whom he loved and served. Still he tried to smile and reassure his father.

Abraham looked at the boy one last time and then turned his head in agony and raised the knife with trembling hands. There was tremendous pain and helplessness. Yet his determination to surrender himself totally to God's will steadied his hands and calmed his heart. He was about to lower the knife on to the tender body of Isaac when he heard the voice of the Lord's messenger, "Do not harm the boy. I know how devoted you are, since you did not withhold from me your own beloved son" (Gen 22:12). God of the unexpected and unimaginable things was doing it again. There again was the promise of blessings, and this time in abundance.

"Do not do this to me, my friend", one might have said when faced with a similar situation. However, Abraham trusted and believed in God. On a human level, Abraham transcended all expressions of trust and faith by his continuous acts of surrender. As a human being he must have experienced tremendous heartache, anxiety and helplessness. His faith was not just a sentimental feeling or a mere act of the mind, but a reality that enabled him to act even in the most challenging situations. No wonder he is called the Father of Faith and stands before us as the towering example of unconditional trust in the promises of the Lord.

The Father will hear the prayer of His beloved Son: "My Father, if it is possible, let this cup pass from me; yet not as I will, but you will" (Mt 26:39). God must have turned to His friend Abraham and said with tears in His eyes, "There will be no sacrificial victim to replace him, because redemption of man requires the sacrifice of my beloved Son".

"If Columbus had turned back, no one would have blamed him. But we would not have remembered him either" – anonymous.

ESAU: "Use It or Lose It"

"So Esau sold Jacob his birthright under oath. Jacob then gave him some bread and the lentil stew; and Esau ate, drank, got up and went his way. Esau cared little for his birthright" (Gen 25: 33-34).

Often people have lost their focus when they began to take things for granted. It is said, "Only when you lose something do you begin to appreciate its true value." That is the story of Esau, whose carelessness led to his downfall from potential greatness.

The birth of the twins was miraculous. Isaac had married Rebekah and waited in expectation for years for a son through whom the blessing promised to Abraham would be handed down. The news of Rebekah's sterility must have been a shock to the couple who wondered how God's promises would come to pass. At the same time this crisis only deepened their faith in God and His power. Isaac, who knew about his mother Sarah's condition and God's hand in his own birth knew God was capable of remedying the situation. The prayer of the faithful couple was answered and Rebekah became pregnant with twins. Even in the womb, they jostled, suggesting greater struggle between them in the future.

Esau, the firstborn, was red and hairy; and Jacob the one who came second was gripping on his heel. Esau grew strong and muscular, and became an expert hunter. He was the favorite of his father and knew he would inherit the blessing as he was the firstborn and possessed the birthright. He loved the company of his father and listened to the stories his father shared while eating the food he prepared. He fancied himself to be the bearer of God's promises and that his descendents would become a great nation. However, he didn't have in him the desire to develop the right relationship with God. He wanted the promised blessings, but was not willing to make any sacrifices on his part to make it a reality.

One day when Esau returned from the open fields, he was taken aback by the delicious smell of his brother's cooking. He was famished and the fact that he had worked long and hard for no catch had made him angry as well. He asked for some of the stew his brother was cooking. At first, Esau felt that Jacob was ignoring him. There was not much communication between the brothers. Esau often looked down upon Jacob as a weakling for his plain appearance and over-attachment to his mother. On the other hand, he considered himself to be the man, due to his strong physique and exceptional hunting abilities.

Jacob looked up from his cooking and promised to give him a bowl of stew under one condition. What Jacob wanted was the birthright, something that was the privilege of the elder son. Just giving the word did not seem to satisfy Jacob as he demanded it under an oath. Esau's hunger was really taking control of his thinking and he felt that he needed to satisfy his physical need by all means. He exaggerated when he stated, "I am on the point of dying. What good will any birthright do me?" (Gen 25: 32). His shrewd brother would not give in to him until he denounced his birthright under oath. Esau ate and drank and walked away fully satisfied. He reassured himself that it did not matter, for he could make more fortunes by his hard work than what the birthright could give. He failed to recognize

God's favor and blessings that were attached to the birthright. By his casual treatment Esau demonstrated the shallowness and carelessness he had for matters of importance.

Though he lost his birthright, he knew since he was his father's favorite that he would still be able to obtain the special blessing. The blessing was the gift of a dying father to his firstborn son that covered different aspects of life: peace, prosperity, wisdom, fertility, long life, victory in battles, and success in life. It was like a legal pronouncement, irrevocable, and honored by God and passed down from generation to generation.

As events unfolded, Jacob deceived Esau once again at the promptings of their mother, and this time Esau lost his father's blessing as well. At this, Esau became both distraught and angry. His desperation was evident as he begged his father, "Father, bless me too!" "Haven't you saved a blessing for me?" "Have you only that one blessing, Father? Bless me too!" (Gen 27: 35). He did not realize that his carelessness had cost him the most important privilege in life.

Esau was livid with rage. He had been tricked twice by this shrewd brother. Not only were these severe blows to his manhood, but also Jacob's tricks deprived him of the family legacy. He realized with grief that it would not be through him that the blessings promised to Abraham and Isaac would be passed on. It was too late now, and Jacob seemed to be enjoying the attention of both the parents. However, Esau did not take responsibility for his failures, but rather blamed his brother's cunningness and his mother's partiality for his miserable condition.

Esau's bruised ego found a solution to end his misery: get rid of Jacob forever. He did not feel himself to be guilty of any misgivings. He failed to recognize that he had not been careful and forthright in his relationship with God and his parents. He had displeased the Lord by selling his birthright. By his marriages to the Canaanite women, he had brought great pain and misery to his parents (Gen 26:34-35). By his actions he had proven himself unworthy to be the successor of the blessings promised to Abraham. Esau was in no mood to recognize his failures and mistakes. Rather, overcome by rage he sought to kill Jacob and possibly redeem the lost privileges.

Once again Rebekah came to Jacob's rescue, who now had the support of Isaac as well and they sent him to his uncle, Laban, Rebekah's brother. They also instructed him not to follow the example of Esau and marry a Canaanite woman. Jacob obeyed his parents and went off to meet Laban, while Esau went ahead and married Mahalath, the daughter of Ishmael. Even Esau's determination to seek revenge seemed to vanish in the course of time and he settled down beyond the Jordan in Edom. Although his lack of enthusiasm in seeking revenge was advantageous to Jacob, Esau proved once again his lack of persistence and perseverance.

Esau seemed to be living for the present without any orientation for the future. He lost his privileged place as a Patriarch of our faith because of his shortsightedness. Esau is remembered for his carelessness. But Jacob, despite his cunningness, stands before us a towering example of perseverance.

Similarly, two men were called by Jesus to be his disciples. Initially, they followed the Lord faithfully. In the end, both committed serious crimes: the first one betrayed the Master and the other denied the Master three times. One looked at himself and found hopelessness; the other eventually looked into the eyes of the Master and found forgiveness. Judas, who betrayed the Master, found only hopelessness within, and would kill himself. Peter, who denied the Master three times, was able to look at Jesus. He would find forgiveness and would reaffirm his love and recommit his life.

How often can carelessness and lack of perseverance deprive us from reaching heights of life that God wants us to reach? How often can short-term goals and the need for immediate gratification blind us from having a true vision for the future?

"The unstable heart is satisfied with his own ways, the good one with his own hard work" (Prov 14:14).

JACOB: Towering Example of Perseverance

"Jacob said, "I will not let you go until you bless me". The angel said, "You shall no longer be spoken of as Jacob, but as Israel, because you have contended with divine and human beings and have prevailed" (Gen 32:27-29).

Human beings are destined for greatness. But one should have a deep aspiration to want it desperately. Jacob wanted it so badly that it separated him from his brother Esau. From the beginning, Jacob tried to develop a relationship with God. Once he knew there was a special purpose for him in life, nothing could stop him from obtaining it.

Esau, Jacob's older brother, proved in time that he was unfit to carry on the responsibilities entailed in the Covenant God had made with Abraham and Isaac. He lived for the moment, with little consideration for the future. God's purposes then would unfold through the younger son, Jacob. One might frown upon the deceitful tactics Jacob employed to accomplish his goals. "How could God let him get away with his shrewdness?" we might wonder. It could be that Jacob had his heart in the right place, and his ultimate goal was to carry on the responsibilities entailed in the Covenant through his life.

God had revealed to Rebekah the future outcome of these two sons: they will represent two nations, the younger one stronger than the older one. Esau was born first and was extremely hairy. Jacob was smooth skinned, born immediately after Esau. The younger one was grasping the heel of his brother, indicating already that he was going to be a hustler for greatness. The two sons grew to be opposites. Esau was a hunter and an outdoorsman who won over the heart of his father, Isaac. Jacob was a quiet person, who loved his mother. It was from his mother that he learned about what God had in store for him and planned to achieve it somehow.

The appropriate moment of bargaining arrived when Esau came home hungry one day. The delicious smell of Jacob's cooking made the famished Esau forget about the significance of his birthright, and he exchanged it for a pot of soup. This contrasting attitude separated these two brothers' destiny. Esau did not care about his dedication to God. His present dire need had such a strong grip on him that he forgot about the significance of his birthright: "The firstborn shall receive a double portion of the inheritance" (Deut 21: 15-17). Esau seemed to be a shallow person, lacking a vision for the future and attaining success. He was not willing to be totally committed to God, as it required deep faith and great sacrifice on his part.

Jacob, who had a vision for the future, cashed in on the opportunity that was presented to him. He now had the birthright, but that was not enough. His mother reminded Jacob that he also needed the blessing from his father Isaac, which would be irrevocable. Isaac, who was old and blind, had intended to give the blessing to the older son Esau. Rebekah carefully laid out a scheme and with shrewdness, succeeded in obtaining the blessings for Jacob from Isaac. Having known God's plan for Jacob, she stood by him courageously and acted shrewdly to ensure that God's plan would unfold through Jacob. She knew that Jacob took important matters in life seriously. Unlike Esau, who lacked appreciation for God and His covenant, Jacob excelled in his dedication to God.

He was greatly strengthened by two wonderful experiences of God, and both of these became moments of blessings for him. One was his powerful dream at Bethel where he saw the ladder, with its foot resting on the ground and the top reaching to the heavens and God's angels were ascending and descending on it. It gave him the awareness of God's constant presence in the world and how his life was continuously influenced by God's principles. The Lord renewed His promises once again with Jacob that involved land, descendants, peace, prosperity and above all His constant presence. Jacob would make a vow to be faithful to God always. As a sign of his vow, he made a shrine and promised to give a tenth of everything to God. Jacob was acknowledging through his actions the essential truth that all that he was and all that he had, originated from God. This was the foundation for Jacob's constant prospering.

The second encounter with the Lord at Jabbok would give Jacob a new identity and greater awareness of God and himself. The struggle with the Angel (or God Himself) proved the resilience and persistence of Jacob. At Jabbok Jacob was wrestled by "some man" until morning. It must have been a fearsome struggle for Jacob. So determined was Jacob that he could not be defeated. Even after dislocating his hips, he would not let the "Man" go until he received a blessing. Jacob was given the new name "Israel", because "you have contended with divine and human beings and have prevailed" (Gen 32:29). The new name, "Israel", which meant "my master", would be a constant reminder to Jacob that he could not gain success by deception, but only by being the humble servant before God the Almighty.

Jacob attained greatness because, unlike his brother Esau, he had a spiritual orientation and vision for the future. Being entirely devoted to God, Jacob served Him faithfully. His gratitude to God was seen by his promise to be always loyal and return a portion of his blessings back to God. He was always humble and yielded to God's commands. Above all, he was a man of persistence who constantly sought God's will and blessings and would not give up until he received them.

At the end of Jacob's struggle with the angel, he was left with a dislocated hip. He walked with a limp. As time went on Jacob must have realized that he could walk upright only with the help of God. Centuries later, another zealous and persistent person would struggle with God on his way to Damascus. Saul, the Pharisee and persecutor of the church, was very determined to destroy the followers of Jesus. As he was knocked down from his horse, he would hear these words, "Saul, Saul, why are you persecuting me?" (Acts 9:4) After that powerful encounter with Jesus, Saul would emerge blind (wounded). His physical blindness would become the first step in curing his spiritual blindness, and he would realize the futility of his efforts to destroy the truth. He would receive a new name, "Paul". He would commit totally to Jesus and proclaim, "It is no longer I who live, but Christ who lives in me" (Gal 2:20).

Though Jacob obtained his birthright and succeeded in receiving the blessing of his father and would become the master of the Promised Land, his acts of deception would catch up with him in different times: twice from his uncle and father-in-law Laban, and from his own children (who would sell the youngest child Joseph as a slave and convince their father that Joseph was killed by the wild animals, and Jacob grieved over this alleged death until the reunion in Egypt). Those experiences would remind Jacob that human actions do have consequences. Jacob would learn the hard way the meaning of the statement, "what goes around comes around". Despite his greatness that he achieved through perseverance, he is remembered for his trickery and deception. Ends, however noble they might be, cannot justify means, if they are evil. Ideally then, we have to be conscious of the means we use to achieve our goals.

"Consider it all joy my brothers and sisters, when you encounter various trials, for you know that the testing of your faith produces perseverance. And let perseverance be perfect, so that you may be perfect and complete, lacking in nothing" (Jas 1:2-4).

JOSEPH: Dreams Come True!

"But now do not be distressed, and do not reproach yourselves for having sold me here. It was really for the sake of saving lives that God sent me here ahead of you" (Gen 45: 5).

Joseph was awakened in the early morning by a dream in a jail in Egypt. He tried to recollect what it was but could not remember it. "Dreams have given me trouble", he said. "Look where I am. I should be with my loving father and my family." As he said this, he sat down on the filthy floor of the jail and lifted his eyes and heart to God whose many blessings and favors he had experienced. Joseph felt the loving presence of God with him constantly and had decided that he would not do anything to offend God.

His thoughts began to drift back to his childhood days. He had always felt so special in the presence of his father. His father loved all of his children, but Joseph being the child in his old age, always received special attention. Jacob's special love and partiality for Joseph aroused jealousy, hatred and rivalry in the hearts of Joseph's brothers. He remembered the beautiful tunic his father had made for him and when he tried to show it to his brothers, he could see anger and resentment in their eyes.

He always had dreams and at times they gave him trouble. He shared his two dreams with his brothers and father: "There we were, binding sheaves in the field, when suddenly my sheaf rose to an upright position, and your sheaves formed a ring around my sheaf and bowed down to it" (Gen 37:6-7); "This time, the sun and the moon and eleven stars were bowing down to me" (Gen 37:9). When he said this, his brothers were outraged and his father began to ponder what his special son would turn out to be. Joseph did not feel condescending or judgmental when he shared the two dreams with them.

Not even in his wildest imagination did he think about the cruelty he would experience at the hands of his brothers. It was heartbreaking even to think that his own brothers wanted to get rid of him by killing him. He thought about how he was thrown into the cistern and how later he was taken out to be sold to the Ishmaelites who took him to Egypt. It was like being rescued from deep waters only to be tossed into the flaming fire. "How could they do such a thing?" he often wondered. It was frightening to be in that cistern; and more frightening to be with these strange merchants. He began to think of his father: "Oh how grief stricken he would be! Will I ever see him again?" Though these thoughts were racing in his mind, he felt a sense of protection, like a shield covering him and a sense of peace began to envelop his whole being. "Oh yes, God is with me and I can feel His presence right here. He is not just present in the land of Canaan. He is everywhere." As he said this aloud he resolved once again to be devoted to God.

God acted mysteriously in his life. He was able to rise in power and gain many privileges with his master. However, when he was enticed by his master's beautiful wife, he was both sad and frightened. Never did he think that she would be so evil as to spread false stories and punish him for his loyalty to his master and above all his faithfulness to his God. He thanked God for giving him the strength to resist the temptation, because she was such a beautiful woman after all. He had no regrets for being in jail as a result of living out his faithfulness to God. It was better to be in jail and be at peace with God than to be in bed with his master's wife and be tormented by the misery of sin. Once again a feeling of peace began to flow through him. He knew God's hands protected him from harm. His master could have put him to death for the alleged crime against his wife. As he sat there on the prison floor, he repeatedly thanked God for His protection.

"But even while he was in prison, the Lord remained with Joseph; He showed him kindness by making the chief jailer well-disposed toward him" (Gen 39:21). Soon Joseph became in charge of all the prisoners in the jail. Dreams that caused him problems now became part of his solution. He won great favors from Pharaoh when he interpreted the dreams about seven years of abundance and seven years of famine. It was very tricky, because he knew if his interpretations were incorrect, he could even lose his life. Joseph trusted in God and interpreted the dreams clearly to Pharaoh. As Pharaoh acted upon Joseph's interpretation, Egypt became the only place where food was available when famine hit the whole world after seven years of abundance.

Joseph was made the second in command after the Pharaoh in Egypt, and felt great joy in being part of alleviating sufferings in these tough times. He began to be hopeful of seeing his family when he saw people from other lands coming to Egypt for food. "How am I going to react if and when God brings them to Egypt?" he thought several times. He now had the power and authority that he could deal with them in any way he wanted. He could make them pay for their cruelties, punish them, put them in jail, or even put them to death. God had given them over to his mercy. But Joseph, having experienced immeasurable love and kindness of God, knew exactly how he was going to act. He knew this was the best opportunity to show them the mercy and the compassion of God and bring them to a greater awareness of God's ways. He only hoped and prayed that they were safe and that his father was still in good health.

Then he saw them one day and immediately recognized them. None of his brothers were aware of his identity. Not even in their wildest dreams could they ever have imagined him in his current position. Joseph played along for some time before revealing his identity. When his brothers realized who he was, they were dumbfounded and startled at the same time. They were afraid of revenge and punishment, and they knew they deserved it.

Joseph assured them that everything happened for a reason. From the evil and wickedness of his brothers, God had brought forth something good. God used Joseph's innocence, faithfulness and dedication to prepare for the security of his family in the time of famine. Joseph would make preparations for all his family to stay comfortably in Egypt. God was acting mysteriously to make them a great nation even in a foreign land.

The innocent Joseph was sold to the Ishmaelites for twenty pieces of silver. His jealous brothers wanted to get rid of Joseph forever. Centuries later, a trusted friend and disciple would betray his Master for thirty pieces of silver. Both actions had brought excruciating pain and suffering to the victims. These capricious acts demonstrated the cruelties of human hearts. God, who is able to bring good out of evil, uses these moments for His purpose. Joseph's slavery status in Egypt would eventually be transformed and become instrumental in securing protection and safety for his starving family. The act of betrayal by Judas would initiate the great sacrifice of Jesus, through which humanity would be gifted with redemption and salvation.

Even in modern families there are acts of betrayal, quarrels, disputes, dysfunctions and divisions. Jealousy, greed, selfish ambition, impatience and intolerance can cause a breach in relationships and turn relatives and friends into enemies. Personal and family vendettas have caused unwarranted bloodshed, made many parents childless, numerous wives widows, and countless children orphans. The only force that can conquer hate, the root of all violence, is the power of love, demonstrated through mercy and forgiveness.

"We know that all things work for good for those who love God, who are called according to His purpose" (Rom 8:28).

MOSES: The Struggle of a Leader

"I cannot carry all these people by myself, for they are too heavy for me. If this is the way you will lead with me, then please do me the favor of killing me at once, so that I need no longer face this distress" (Num 11:14-15).

With the help of Joseph, the whole household of Jacob had settled down in Egypt. God blessed them and they grew in large numbers. Things were going pretty well for them until fear and insecurity got the best of the new Pharaoh who knew nothing about Joseph and the history of the Hebrews. He sought to suppress them through various forms of oppression that included forced labor and the killing of the newborn Hebrew male infants. Their cry reached God and He remembered His Covenant with Abraham and his descendants. The appropriate divine time was at hand for God to act upon His promises.

A young Hebrew woman kept her newborn baby boy hidden for some time before placing him in the presence of Pharaoh's daughter. God touched her heart and guided her actions. She took the boy and gave it to a Hebrew woman, his own mother, for nursing. When he grew up, she brought him to Pharaoh's daughter, who adopted him and gave him the name Moses. He grew up as an Egyptian and led a comfortable life in the palace of the Pharaoh.

As time went on, Moses became aware of his identity and family origins. The visit to his kinsmen reassured him that he had to help his people even if it meant leaving his familiar and comfortable life in the palace. He began to be enraged at the forced labor and cruel punishment that were inflicted upon the Hebrews. Right before his eyes was an Egyptian kicking a Hebrew slave with great force and flogging him mercilessly with a whip that had many pieces of tiny, sharp bones strapped to it. The agonizing cry of the Hebrew as the whip tore into his flesh sent Moses into a frenzy and drawing his sword, he slew the Egyptian instantly. When reality set in he quickly hid the body of his victim. He was surprised to witness the next day the quarrel of two Hebrews. He thought to himself, "How can these people fight among themselves when they have a common enemy inflicting constant punishment?" He was horrified at their sneer, "Who has appointed you ruler and judge over us? Are you thinking of killing me as you killed the Egyptian?" (Ex 2:14). For a moment, fear gripped Moses' heart and he knew fleeing from Egypt was the only form of escape.

Running away from Egypt, he went to Midian where he found a home and began a new life. He tried hard to put all the events of his past out of his mind. Moses was tending the flock of his father-in-law Jethro, when he encountered the Lord at the burning bush at Horeb. As he witnessed the amazing sight, Moses had no idea that his destiny was about to change forever. The Lord revealed His identity as the God of Abraham, Isaac and Jacob, and the mission He had in store for Moses: "Bring my afflicted people from the land of slavery to the land of freedom, a land flowing with milk and honey" (Ex 3:4-10). Moses, overwhelmed by this powerful experience and insurmountable task, frantically searched for excuses as to why he was not the right person. Moses was afraid to go back to Egypt. He felt that he was inadequate and incompetent for such a noble task. God turned down all his excuses and gave him an assistant, Aaron, Moses' own brother. Upon Moses' request God revealed the divine name as "I AM WHO AM" (Ex 3:14), and assured him of His constant presence, protection and the victory of his mission.

Moses and Aaron stood boldly before Pharaoh and demanded, "Let my people go" (Ex 5:1). The angered Pharaoh made a mockery of the demand and inflicted added punishment upon the Hebrews as if to show Moses that he was in command, not some unknown God. God's power was manifested through Moses through many signs and wonders, but still Pharaoh did not budge. The plagues became intolerable for Pharaoh and the Egyptians but they left the households of the Hebrews unharmed. At the end of the tenth plague that caused the death of all the firstborn in Egypt, Pharaoh reluctantly released the Hebrews to be on their way. Jubilant in their state of freedom, the Hebrews celebrated the Passover and set out on their journey to the Promised Land.

The overjoyed Israelites were on their way to the Promised Land singing songs of praise to the almighty God who liberated them from slavery and gave them freedom. The galloping sound of the horses and war cries disrupted their festive mood as they saw in horror the army of Pharaoh closing in on them! Alas they were by then at the bank of the Red Sea, and ahead of them were the deep waters and behind them was the cruel army of Pharaoh. Moses began to hear the complaints of the people. "Why have you brought us out? We want to go back, so we won't be killed. It is better to be a slave than a corpse".

Moses assured them of God's mighty power. God would be with them in this battle and give them victory. The power of God was revealed as Moses, at God's word, lifted his staff and stretched his hands over the sea and it parted. The people crossed over through the parted sea, and once they reached the other side witnessed the destruction and drowning of Pharaoh's army right before them. "This will convince the people and they will trust in God's power", Aaron told Moses, who looked very skeptical.

They reached Mount Sinai and God revealed Himself to the people. He was set to give them the Ten Commandments that would help them become the holy people through whom the Promised Messiah would come into the world. God ratified His Covenant with the people and they said in one accord "We will do everything that the Lord has told us" (Ex 24:3).

God commanded Moses to come up the mountain to receive the stone tablets on which God had lovingly written the Ten Commandments. The forty days and nights that Moses spent with the Lord intensified his love for Him. It was like two friends sharing their ideas, dreams and hopes for people entrusted to their care. While God and Moses were engrossed in planning a peaceful life for the people, there were strange things happening among them. How short-lived was their memory! How quick were they to forget about the stupendous power of God and to their shame, give themselves over to idolatry! The breaking of the first commandment by worshiping the golden calf was just the beginning of their constant struggle with God and Moses.

Troubles were endless for Moses. The disbelief of the people in God became severe when they were thirsty, hungry, or longing for bread and meat. Constantly they rebelled against God and accused Moses of bringing them out into the wilderness to die. Even though they had witnessed God's stupendous power, they failed to trust Him completely to provide for their needs. Instead they constantly murmured, complained and rebelled. The difficult moments during their journey to the Promised Land should have been an opportune time to renew their dependency on God. Instead, they became moments of rebellion that even led to the abandonment of the true God for other gods.

Even when God's wrath flared up against them to the extent of destroying them (Ex 32:10; Num 21:4-9), Moses found himself constantly pleading for these ungrateful people. He could have let God destroy these stiff-necked and rebellious people, but constantly he pleaded for God's mercy and forgiveness upon them. Even the greatest leader with the best intentions, ideas, motivations and commitment can become susceptible to discouragement and desperation when he is unjustly criticized and his orders neglected. Overcome by desperation and disappointment over the people's behavior, Moses asked the Lord to take his life: "….please do me the favor of killing me at once, so that I no longer need to face this distress" (Num 11:15). Frustration, discouragement, pain, disappointment, anger and anguish were evident in this plea of Moses. God, who totally understood the turbulent feelings of Moses, ignored his request and asked him to select Seventy Elders as his helpers.

Moses — who enjoyed a very special friendship with God; who led the people out of slavery; who endured tremendous heartaches due to the unfaithfulness of the people — was deprived of the privilege of entering the Promised Land. Numbers 20:2-13 describes the scene of bitter complaints of the people for water, God's specific instruction, and Moses' act of disobedience due to his frustration. God had instructed Moses to speak to the rock to bring out water. Moses out of frustration struck the rock twice and water gushed out. This is seen as Moses' sin since it was contrary to God's instruction. Moses was allowed to view the Promised Land only from the mountain top.

We might wonder if God was too harsh on Moses. God must have held Moses to a higher standard than anyone else. Moses' act of disobedience was more than a personal sin, as all of his actions had a witness value. God could not allow Moses to set a bad example before the people and let him get away with. He was allowed to see the Promised Land from the top of a mountain. However, Moses died as a contented man, having accomplished many wonderful things for the people.

Could we also think that while God was stern with Moses, He stored a surprise for him as well? The Promised Land would eventually be seen as a representation of the true home, the Heavenly Jerusalem, towards which we all travel in faith to meet God face to face. Could it be that God punished Moses by not permitting him to enter the earthly Promised Land, but showed the richness of His mercy and compassion by taking him to the true home, the Heavenly Jerusalem!

We will see Moses again at the top of a mountain. This time he will be with the Prophet Elijah, conversing with Jesus at the scene of Transfiguration (Mk 9:4).

"A grateful heart makes life joyful. True joy is always out of reach for an ungrateful person" – author

JOSHUA:
"On the Battlefield for the Lord"

"If it does not please you to serve the Lord, decide today whom you will serve...... As for me and my household, we will serve the Lord" (Josh 24:15).

Joshua was very determined to serve the Lord from the beginning. He had heard of God's Covenant, and when Moses burst forth onto the scene with the cry "Let my people go", he knew God was acting upon His promises. The events that followed were like a dream. He witnessed God's mighty power many times and was convinced that the living and true God would lead the people to the Promised Land by removing all obstacles in their path. Joshua never imagined that he himself was destined to lead the people.

If someone had told him earlier about leading the people to the Promised Land, he would have laughed at it. Because he knew of only one leader, and that was Moses. He always marveled at the friendship and closeness Moses seemed to enjoy with God. Many a time he was saddened at all the trouble people gave to Moses. The people seemed to have short memories, like children who often concentrate on their present need, forgetting everything that was done for them in the past. The fearsome anger Moses exhibited at times frightened Joshua, but he knew that his leader was acting out of frustration because of the ungrateful acts of a stiff-necked people. He vowed to be faithful to God, never straying from His path and to be always loyal to Moses.

He cried bitterly when he learned Moses would not be with them to take possession of the Promised Land! He never doubted God's ways, but it was only natural for him to feel tremendous sadness and loss of his beloved leader. The responsibilities at hand made him forget about this personal loss and he wanted to be at the service of his Lord and God. He knew that people respected him and believed in his capabilities. He knew every single person as they all set off together from Egypt. The vast majority of them had died due to their rebellious actions and unfaithfulness. He knew every single newborn and prayed that they would be different.

He was apprehensive about the task at hand, although he firmly believed that God's hand would guide him. It was the people who gave him anxious moments and sleepless nights. He knew how easily they could turn their backs on God. There were some who constantly complained and murmured about everything, making even the honest ones go astray. For some, the best plans, intentions and actions of the leader were not ever good enough. But the task at hand demanded not doubt or self-pity, but resolute determination to carry out God's commands. He gathered the crowd and moved on. God's mighty power was upon him, enabling him to work signs and wonders like his great predecessor Moses did.

Their greatest challenge was ahead of them to conquer Jericho, a well-established city with a mighty wall and a powerful army. The inhabitants of Jericho believed that no power on earth or heaven would be able to defeat them. But there was an air of fear when they heard about the Israelites advancing towards them led by a fearsome leader Joshua. What frightened them even more was a rumor that the

Hebrews were led by their living God, who performed many wondrous signs in Egypt. Consequently they were always on the lookout for any strangers in the city.

God often does extra-ordinary things and uses unlikely people. In this case, the one who came to the aid of the spies for Joshua was Rahab, the harlot. She protected the Hebrew spies from the king and helped them to complete their mission. Her sole request was for the safety of her family during the battle, as a favor in return, which Joshua would grant her at the end.

Joshua knew that his military power was not enough to conquer the enemy. The greatest power, he knew, came from God the Almighty. The Ark of the Covenant reminded them of the constant presence and power of God. Joshua knew that the only way to capture the city was by following the commands of the Lord. God gave him instructions as to how they should circle the city with the Ark of the Lord for seven days. It sounded like an unlikely military strategy. But Joshua wholeheartedly trusted in God's commands. He did not reveal to the people God's instructions all at once, but little by little. The selected troops marched ahead, followed by seven priests carrying rams horns, followed by priests carrying the Ark, the rear guard, and finally the people. They were to circle the city once a day for six days. On the seventh day they were to march seven times and then at a long blast of the rams horns, they were to shout out loud.

Joshua demanded perfect silence from all. The only noise allowed was the blowing of the horns. Joshua knew that marching once for the six days and seven times on the seventh day would make people doubt his plans and God's power. It wouldn't be long before someone suggested the futility and insanity of the whole affair. He knew then it would grow from a murmur into shouts of rebellion. He sternly ordered them to keep their mouths shut so that they would not imitate the sins of their fathers.

After a few days of witnessing this strange phenomenon, the inhabitants of Jericho might have been amused. But Joshua knew that God would give them victory if they followed His commands. At the end of the seventh round there was the horn blast and Joshua urged the people to shout aloud. At the tremendous shout of the people the walls of Jericho crumbled and they witnessed the awesome power of God.

The conquest of the Promised Land was not an easy task. A number of times Joshua experienced failures like Moses due to the faithlessness of his people. Like Moses, he constantly challenged them to make the Lord their choice. He attributed every military victory to the Lord and the new territories they occupied as God's gifts.

Joshua was convinced that the acquisition of the Promised Land was not the end of God's promises. It was an indication of how serious God was about the Covenant He made with their fathers and with the people at Mount Sinai. God had promised Abraham that through him all the nations of the world would be blessed. The newly formed tiny nation was to become a sign of God's plan for the world, as it was through her (Israel) that God was going to unfold His plan of salvation for the whole world. It was through Israel, the newly formed tiny nation, that God would send the promised Savior. It was imperative then for the people to be faithful and loyal to God and His statutes, commandments, and decrees. Joshua challenged them to decide for themselves who they would serve. He made his intention clear when he said, "As for me and my household, we will serve the Lord" (Josh 24:15).

Joshua believed in the power of God and relied upon His strength to accomplish his goals. There are times in our lives, when even the best laid plans and preparations might not lead us to succeed in reaching our goals. Human capabilities, though noble in many ways, are at the same time insignificant when we compare them to the power and might of God. However, when human abilities are guided by the grace and power of the almighty God, we are assured of victory in the battles of life.

"Trust Him. Ultimately, it is the Lord who wins your battles."
– author

RUTH: Blessed Beyond Imagination

"Boaz took Ruth. When they came together as man and wife, the Lord enabled her to conceive and she bore a son...... They called him Obed. He was the father of Jesse, the father of David" (Ruth 4:13-17).

Sometimes life can take one to places and situations that one could hardly imagine. Could Ruth, a Moabite woman, a Gentile according to the biblical norms, have ever imagined that she would be remembered lovingly and with great admiration centuries after her life? Better still, could she ever have hoped to be connected with the family of the great Israelite, King David? Greater still, had she ever realized that she was going to be part of God's plan of salvation for human beings, that she would become an ancestress of Jesus, the Savior of the world? She became part of the ancestry of Jesus through her filial piety and devotion. Through her dedication and faithfulness, she communicated the greatest good news to the whole world – God's universal love and gift of salvation.

Unimaginable things can happen to a person who places absolute trust in the Lord. The story of Ruth bears witness to that. It was only through God's plan that two persons, Naomi and Ruth, born and raised in two different countries and cultures could come together to accomplish His purpose. Naomi and her husband Elimelech and their two sons Mahlon and Chilion lived a comfortable life until famine hit the land of Bethlehem. Collecting all their possessions, they departed for the land of Moab, where there was food. Naomi became a widow after a few years. Her two sons then married two beautiful women of Moab: Orpah and Ruth.

Tragedies seemed to continue in Naomi's life as both of her sons died unexpectedly, leaving the two beautiful Moabite women widows. There they were – three widows wondering about their future with little support from anyone. Naomi knew that she was approaching the sunset of her life, but her young daughters-in-law had long lives ahead of them. Knowing that she would not be able to take care of them, she urged them to return to their people. She really loved them, but realized that she was helpless in every way to offer the help they needed. She only wished and prayed for their security and happiness. She knew that Orpah and Ruth could return to their homes, probably remarry and have children and secure lives.

Orpah unwillingly agreed; however, Ruth refused. The words that immortalized Ruth came from her great love and devotion to Naomi. Ruth said, "Do not ask me to abandon or forsake you! For wherever you go I will go, wherever you lodge, I will lodge, your people shall be my people and your God my God" (Ruth 1:16). What powerful words from Ruth, a young gentile widow, totally willing to abandon her life and face the unknown! She was willing to give up her homeland, her people and her religion to support her helpless mother-in-law and to serve her God. The words of Ruth would become the hallmark of her pledge of loyalty, which would be favorably rewarded by God beyond her imagination.

Ruth might not have come to this conclusion overnight. She must have considered herself fortunate to be married to a wonderful person who was devoted to her in every way. She assumed that he had learned this dedication from his parents, who were devoted to one another. There was great affection and respect among all the members of this Hebrew family. What touched her the most was their dedication to their God. It was only natural for Ruth to come to the conclusion that their obedience to their God was the reason behind their blameless lives. Even great calamities and misfortunes in life never seemed to shake their trust in Him. It was natural for Ruth then to inquire more and more about their God and slowly come to the realization that the living God would extend His love and mercy even to her. Deep within her, there was this great conviction that there was a purpose in her life and that could be actualized only by her faithfulness to Him.

She was stepping out in faith to face the unknown. Although it was rather painful to leave the familiar shore and set out onto the unknown waters, a sense of God's presence calmed her fears and anxieties. She trusted and believed that everything happened according to God's plan even when the plan was not very clear to her.

They reached Bethlehem in time for harvest. When the women asked, "can this be Naomi?", we can feel the anguish and pain in Naomi's response, "Do not call me Naomi, (amiable). But call me Mara, for the almighty has made it bitter for me. I went away with an abundance, but the Lord has brought me back destitute" (Ruth 1:20-21). True, Naomi went away with abundance and in the company of her husband and two sons. She came back destitute, only in the company of Ruth, a humble girl, whose loyalty now gave her strength. Even though there was anguish in her heart, she came to the realization that the loyalty of Ruth could open up possibilities of a better life for both of them. Naomi had left Bethlehem at a time of famine (nothingness), but came back at a time of harvest (abundance). The abundance of blessings would be reaped through the dedication of Ruth.

Ruth soon gained the attention of Boaz, a wealthy landowner and kinsman of Naomi, and this eventually led to their marriage. Their son Obed would become the grandfather of King David. What they hoped for was less in comparison to what God had in store for both of them. God richly rewarded the unwavering commitment of Ruth. Her life clearly proclaimed that God's blessings were not restricted to one nation or to certain people, but for all people who would acknowledge Him as their God.

Ruth's story is a beautiful portrayal of faithfulness on the part of all the leading characters portrayed in this book. Noami showed her care and faithfulness when she urged Ruth to return to the safety of her home, remarry and begin a new life. Ruth, on the other hand, was dedicated to her old and helpless mother-in-law and wanted to serve her and her God. Boaz was willing to redeem the family's land and marry the helpless Moabite widow. God, who saw it all, blessed their faithfulness beyond their imagination: Ruth and Boaz became part of God's Covenant and ancestors of Jesus, the Savior of the world.

"Life presents numerous opportunities to make it sublime. Blessed is the one who sees and holds on to God's hidden hands and makes the best of those opportunities" – author.

SAUL: Great Start, but Sad End

"The Spirit of the Lord had departed from Saul, and he was tormented by an evil spirit" 1 Sam 16:14.

The people of Israel looked around and found that neighboring nations were ruled by kings. They, on the other hand, had Prophets and Judges. Though they conceptually believed God to be their king, they were impressed by the organizational structure of neighboring monarchies. The famous judge Samuel had led the people according to God's statutes and decrees. Previously there were many God-fearing Prophets and Judges who constantly reminded the people that they were people of the Covenant, and that God would accomplish His special purpose for humanity through them. Samuel, the holy man of God, had done just that. He was getting old and hoped that his sons would live for the people as he had dedicated his life to them.

However, human weaknesses and sinful attractions got the best of Samuel's sons and they strayed from righteous living. It was like the evil corrupting the head and making the whole body ill as a result. The elders of the people who had seen the benefits of living according to God's ways approached their favorite old Judge with a demand for a king. Samuel was heartbroken at seeing the failures of his sons and at the same time displeased at the request to have a king. He knew this would lead them away from being God's people and lead them towards being a worldly power. When Samuel prayed to God, He granted their request, but with a warning of the difficulties associated with earthly kings: forced military drafting, taxation, possible tyranny, and exploitation.

But the people were resolute in their request. God did not force them to change their minds, but granted their request.

God was pleased with Saul, a member of the tribe of Benjamin. Saul exhibited great physical qualities and godly traits. "There was no other Israelite more handsome than Saul; he stood head and shoulders above other people" (1 Sam 9:2). He was very devoted to his father and his family. He believed in the power of God and acknowledged that God could speak through His spokespersons like Samuel. It came as no surprise when he anointed Saul as the first king of Israel. God also provided many signs to Samuel that confirmed that Saul should be the king. At that moment, Saul was the best person for this important task.

Saul was anointed by Samuel and God's spirit rushed upon him. Saul gained the confidence and admiration of the people, and with the help of God, he achieved many victories in battle. Samuel stepped down as the leader of Israel and he encouraged the people to be faithful to God at all times and to support their new king.

Saul's faithfulness to God did not last too long. He thought he was in command and decided to overstep boundaries that included taking over religious duties which displeased the Lord. Saul's disobedience to God also became visible when he ignored the explicit command received through Samuel, who wanted to have everything destroyed with the Amalekites (1 Sam 15). Saul, on the other hand, spared the king of Amalek, Agag, and the best of his fat sheep, oxen and lambs. He wanted to take the king as a military prisoner and declare his power before all. Looking at the fat sheep, oxen and lambs, he must have thought he could make much greater use of them (including sacrifice) than complete destruction. Contrary to God's instruction Saul wanted to store up the wealth and riches from the defeated nation.

Saul gradually slipped away from God and he was losing God's spirit due to his disobedience. In place of God's spirit was an evil spirit, probably violent rage resulting from his jealousy, constantly tormenting him. When Saul took matters into his hands, contrary to specific instructions given to him, he was replacing God's purposes with his goals. He forgot what his responsibilities were, and sought after his personal gratification.

Saul's heart was tormented by a spirit of melancholy and depression. He had found temporary comfort in the skillful music played by David. No physical comforts and pleasures of life could give him lasting contentment. Human beings experience constant restlessness when they get separated from God and that was Saul's story. Centuries later, St. Augustine would paraphrase this principle, "Our hearts are made for you O Lord; they are restless until they rest in you".

The worst came when jealousy gripped the heart of Saul with the arrival of David. To make matters worse, the Philistines became stronger under their new hero Goliath. Having lost the presence of the Spirit of God within him, Saul was gripped with fear. Up until then, God's power had reassured Saul of victory in many battles. His own physical power did not match his giant opponent, Goliath. When David stepped forward to meet the challenge, Saul was concerned about the boy's safety and offered him his armor. However, David moved ahead with his God-given confidence and slings in his hand. David trusted more in the Lord than the armor of Saul, and surrendered his heart to God's power.

The killing of Goliath by David should have been an occasion for great celebration, but soon turned out to be a moment of rage for the king. The women's song, "Saul has slain his thousands and David his ten thousands" (1 Sam 18:7) annoyed Saul to such an extent that he wanted to kill David. Soon Saul the king became captive of his own evil feelings, totally forgetting the reason why he was chosen by God to be the king. Though David later on became his son-in-law and close friend of his son, Jonathan, nothing stopped Saul from his wicked desire to exterminate David. He had sold his soul to the devil and faced the tragic end.

Saul had a great start. He was courageous, charismatic, humble and capable initially. Everything was going right for him as long as he remained faithful to the Lord. When he separated himself from the source of his life and nourishment, his life became miserable and a failure and eventually it withered away. As a result, Saul experienced in his life a loss of fervor and lack of purpose. What was sad in this case was that Saul did not even realize that he was losing God's spirit.

Revelation 3:20 reads, "Behold, I stand at the door and knock. If anyone hears my voice and opens the door, I will enter his house and dine with him, and he with me". God stands at the door of every person's heart, waiting to be invited. God does not force His way into a person's life. Even when He is invited, His Spirit remains in a person only as long as He feels wanted. Whenever God's spirit experienced neglect and rejection in human life, He gracefully would move out.

"I am the vine, you are the branches. Whoever remains in me and I in him will bear much fruit, because without me you can do nothing" (Jn 15:5).

DAVID: "A Man after God's own Heart"

"David strengthened himself in the Lord his God" (1 Sa 30:6)

God provided the best available person to serve His people. Saul was chosen as the king because he was the best available. When Saul turned his back on God, He looked for the next best available in Israel. His eyes fell upon David the shepherd boy, son of Jesse from Bethlehem. Nothing happens by chance with God. The election of David to be the king of Israel meant God was acting upon His promises, gradually unfolding His plan for the true, good shepherd king.

The shepherd boy, David, grew up to be one of the greatest personalities in the history of Israel. He is portrayed as the ideal king, powerful warrior, great musician, Psalmist, a sinner and a 'saint'. It was from his family the Savior of the world would come. Often when people would dream of the promised Messiah, they imagined someone like David, who would restore pride, peace and prosperity in the kingdom. The best compliment came from God Himself who said, "David is a man after my own heart" (Acts 13:12; cf. 1 Sam 13:13-14).

David had a dream start. He was very handsome and talented. He was chosen by God as the king to succeed Saul. He was anointed by Samuel and would soon find himself in the court of Saul. Eventually, he became a national hero when he killed the Philistine giant Goliath. As the spirit of God was with David, he went on to become the king of Israel and to win many battles.

One of the persons in the bible to face some of the greatest troubles in life was David. His troubles started when Saul became jealous of him and his fame. He had to escape several assassination attempts, leave his homeland and hide in the wilderness and even among strangers. Seeds of jealousy and resentment were planted in Saul's heart when he heard the women of Israel lavishing praises upon David, "Saul has slain his thousands, and David his tens of thousands" (1 Sam 18:7). Soon resentment began to grow in Saul's heart and he viewed David as a rival and enemy.

When one does not have the power of God within oneself, insecurities, rage and doubts conquer one's heart. Saul, pierced with jealousy, sought to kill David, whose valor had saved the kingdom from the wrath of the Philistines. He plotted to have David killed by the Philistines (1 Sam 18:20-27); Saul made his intention of killing David clear to his son Jonathan (David's dear friend) and the servants (1 Sam 19:1). Even after David became a refugee, Saul searched for him with his army in order to kill him (1 Sam 24:1-3).

On the other hand, David demonstrated great character and loyalty to God when he refused to kill Saul even though he had two opportunities (1 Sam 24:5-6; 26:8-12). David always acknowledged Saul as God's anointed (1 Sam 26:9-10) and refused to harm Saul who was constantly seeking to kill him. The situations and circumstances were just right to end his sufferings and fugitive status. The words of the servants were compelling, "God has delivered your enemy into your hands" (1 Sam 24:5). David could have seized the moment and could have killed Saul. There would have been no one to resent his action. The people who were miserable under

Saul would have acclaimed David as their king immediately, but David did not take matters into his hands and commit the evil of inflicting harm upon God's anointed. David's integrity and character were clear in his words and actions: "The Lord forbid that I should do such a thing to my master, the Lord's anointed. With these words David restrained his men and would not permit them to attack Saul" (1 Sam 24:7-8). David wept when he heard about the death of Saul and Jonathan and he wrote an elegy for them. It was like David was already living out the true dimension of love: "Love your enemies and pray for those who persecute you".

Even after David had unified all the tribes of Israel and established himself as the sovereign king, he always remained humble before God. He constantly remembered that his strength came from the Lord. When David brought the Ark of the Covenant to Jerusalem, he danced with joy like a common man in the sight of all. He was not crestfallen when he was denied the request to build the temple and graciously accepted the fact that he had shed too much blood (1 Chr 22:7-9). He always trusted in the Lord his God and surrendered his life totally to Him.

Even David's great sins in his personal life have a moral lesson for all. He committed adultery with Bathsheba and plotted the murder of her husband Uriah. He committed two of the greatest sins: adultery and murder. Consumed by lustful passion, he committed the horrible sin of adultery. To hide his heinous sin, he plotted the murder of the innocent Uriah. Confronted with the reality of his sin, he was stricken by guilt and shame. But these sins and subsequent feelings of guilt did not destroy David as he exhibited true remorse and repentance. "A clean heart create for me, God; renew within me a steadfast spirit" (Ps 51), demonstrated his true contrition and desire to turn away from sin. Having experienced God's merciful love, David did not allow the troubles of life to destroy him. He faced the consequences of his sins courageously.

He had to face the death of his child, born from the adulterous relationship with Bathsheba. In his own home, his son Ananon raped his daughter Tamar; Ananon then was killed by his other son Absolom. Absolom later revolted against his father. Then to the great grief of David, Absolom himself was killed. The one closest to the Lord had endured a great number of trials!

Unlike Saul, setbacks and problems never destroyed David. He never abandoned God. There may have been moments when his passion made him forget about God, but he never abandoned Him. Whenever this great person faces troubles, it became a moment to renew his strength and trust in the Lord. 1 Samuel 30:6 reads, "David strengthened himself in the Lord His God." The selection from 1 Samuel 30:1-6 has the context in which David arrived in Ziklag fleeing from Saul. He found that Ziklag had been raided by the Amalekites, leaving it in ruin and taking all the people captive. Among the captives were his own wives Ahinoam and Abigail. All were grief-stricken, but soon David became the target of the frustration and anger of the men around him who wanted to stone and kill him, because he was not there when he was needed the most. Here is where the end of the 6th verse becomes a source of light for every person who has ever faced troubles: "David strengthened himself in the Lord his God."

As David renewed his strength in the Lord, he was able to face all the trials and tribulations of his life. In every situation David always came back to the source of his strength, the strength of his life – God Himself. Different psalms that are attributed to David give us an indication of this aspect of his life. David did not try to solve the problems in his life by his own strength. Rather, he relied on the Lord.

Troubles in life can make one a better person or a bitter person. Troubles, inevitable in human life, can come unexpectedly or as a result of one's choices. They can be inflicted by others, inherited in life, be the result of great crisis or unwarranted calamities, or could even have no logical explanation. In David's case, troubles made him a better person as he constantly sought to renew his strength in the Lord.

"Though I walk in the valley of darkness, I fear no evil, for you are with me; your rod and your staff give me courage" *(Ps 23:4).*

SOLOMON: Young and Wise….. but?

"When Solomon was old, his wives had turned his heart to strange gods, and his heart was not entirely with the Lord, as the heart of his father David had been" (1 Kg 11:4).

From the perspective of worldly comfort, prestige and prosperity, Solomon's period of kingship was greater than any other time for Israel, including the reign of his father David. Solomon was born as if with a silver spoon in his mouth. He enjoyed all the comforts of the palace. Though David's sin of adultery and murder cast a gloom over the whole nation, his repentance and penance had made people forget about his failure and embrace the newborn with great joy. Solomon was truly loved by his parents David and Bathsheba and all the people. He admired his father David greatly, both for his military power and devotion to his people. But what left the greatest impression in his heart was the unchanging devotion his father had towards the living God. Though his father had a fair amount of trouble in his life, he always seemed to renew his strength in the Lord.

Though his stepbrother Adonijah plotted to be crowned as the king, their father favored Solomon. It was part of God's plan that Solomon would succeed his father (1 Chr 22: 9), and nothing could change that plan. David blessed and instructed Solomon with these words: "Take courage and be a man. Keep the mandates of the Lord, your God, following His ways and observing His statutes, commands, ordinances and decrees as they are written in the law of Moses, that you may succeed in whatever you do and wherever you turn" (1 Kg 2: 2-3).

Solomon vowed to be faithful to God. He wanted to be a fair and just ruler for his people. He was blessed with a great dream in which God asked him to request any favor that He could grant Solomon. Solomon's faithfulness and intentions were fully portrayed in his request. He humbly asked, "O Lord, my God, you have made me your servant, to succeed my father David, but I am a mere youth, I do not know at all how to act. I serve you in the midst of the people whom you have chosen, a people so vast that it cannot be numbered or counted. Give your servant, therefore, an understanding heart to judge your people and to distinguish right from wrong". (1 Kg 3: 7-9).

What an awesome prayer! Solomon showed maturity and insight beyond his age to make such a request. God was highly pleased at this and granted his request and more. God's generosity knew no boundaries and His blessings for Solomon were abundant. At the outset, God commanded Solomon to be loyal and devoted to Him. Solomon exhibited great wisdom in his life, as he had the ability to distinguish between right and wrong. He ruled the people fairly and his name and fame spread to the whole world. Peace and prosperity were the earmarks of his period and the time of his reign was known as the golden age of Israel.

He was given the greatest privilege of all: to build the temple of the Lord. Though David desired to build the temple, it was Solomon who God chose to carry out this task. David had fought many wars and solidified the nation.

He had brought the Ark of the Lord to Jerusalem. The construction of the first temple gave the people a sense of identity and great pride. The temple became the new sign of God's Covenant with His people. Solomon dedicated devoutly the House of the Lord and made a peace offering to the Lord: twenty thousand oxen and one hundred and twenty thousand sheep. He felt grateful in making these huge offerings and vowed once again to remain faithful to God forever.

Occasionally we hear people say, "I was young and stupid". In Solomon's case, one could easily say, "he was young and wise, but became old and stupid". Normally, experiences in life and age help people to correct mistakes and to make better choices. In the case of Solomon, the opposite was true. Twice the Lord had appeared to him and promised His blessings upon Solomon. He also had given ample warning not to go away from His protection and stoop down to worship foreign gods. Eventually, Solomon forgot God's blessings and warnings.

The demise of Solomon was a classic example of how one can fall from the state of greatness to total ruin. Ignorance could not be seen as an excuse for his situation, as he was the wisest living person. Solomon, with his gift of wisdom, could discern right and wrong, but somehow did not possess prudence or character to practice it constantly in his life. Somehow Solomon replaced his love and dedication for God with other realities of life.

Solomon's marriages with the foreign women took his heart away from God. Having had the great experiences of the Divine in his life and having enjoyed abundant favors from God, Solomon should have been the true instrument of bringing his pagan wives to the true faith in the living God. Solomon failed miserably, first by tolerating their pagan practices; eventually compromising with them in his life; and finally embracing them for himself. Solomon committed the abominable sin – idolatry.

God still did not give up His plan for the salvation of the human race. The natural consequence of Solomon's sin was the downfall of his kingdom that eventually became divided. The divided kingdom was a true portrayal of Solomon's divided heart in his old age. Yet God preserved Judah and Jerusalem for the sake of fulfilling His promise – the promised Messiah would be born through the family of David.

Three realities of life that can make or break a person are power, money and love (specifically, lust of a man for woman or vice versa). They are true blessings if they are used wisely according to one's situation. They can become evil and take control over a person and make him a slave if one fails to have control over them. All of Solomon's wisdom did not help him when he became a slave to his passions. In his old age, he gave in to the conniving and manipulative ways of his foreign wives. His devotion became divided as he began to focus more on himself than on God or the people God entrusted to his care.

Money, power and love are realities that can be used for one's selfish purposes or for the good of oneself and others and ultimately for the glory of God. When the focus is shifted from God and others to totally oneself, these realities can enslave a human person and deprive him/her from realizing the true meaning of human life.

"No one can serve two masters. He will either hate one and love the other, or be devoted to one and despise the other. You cannot serve God and mammon" (Mt 7:24).

JONAH: A Jealous Prophet?

"This is why I fled at first to Tarshish. I knew that you are a gracious and merciful God, slow to anger, rich in clemency, loathe to punish. And now, Lord, please take my life from me; for it is better for me to die than to live" (Jon 4:2-3).

Jonah was pretty happy to be God's spokesperson. He loved giving God's messages, especially those that were in line with fire and brimstone. Constantly he demanded from the people the need for conversion and repentance. He wanted his people to walk in God's ways. However, he was very careful to avoid those people outside of his Hebrew tradition. To him, others were worthless and destined to be destroyed. He could not wait to see when only God's chosen, holy people would survive and thrive in the world.

It came as a great shock to Jonah, when he was commanded by the Lord to go to Nineveh, the traditional enemy city of Israel. Jonah loathed the inhabitants of Nineveh and had heard of their sinful lives. Secretly he must have prayed many times that they be destroyed with all their wickedness, because he did not want his people to be influenced by their lawlessness and impurity. It would have been wonderful if God had called him to witness the destruction of the city, but God's message here looked like a mere warning. Many times Jonah could not fathom God's ways, especially when it came to His boundless mercy that He seemed to offer to all who called upon Him. If it were to be left to Jonah, Nineveh and its inhabitants would have been destroyed a long time ago. "Well", Jonah thought, "the best thing to do is to go away from the Lord in the opposite direction." So he set out for Tarshish.

Jonah was peacefully sleeping when a violent storm began to rock the boat. There was absolute chaos and all were calling upon their gods to rescue them from peril. The captain might have been enraged to see one of the boarders fast asleep instead of calling for help. When Jonah told them about the whole situation and how he ended up on the ship and from whom he was running, the whole crew was frightened. They seemed to exhibit more awe and fear for the living God than Jonah himself. The only option he was able to come up with was to tell them to toss him off the boat into the sea. The goodwill of the crewmembers who were gentiles was very visible as they tried hard to steady the ship and thereby save Jonah. However, nothing seemed to work and they reluctantly agreed to cast Jonah into the sea. They implored God's mercy for their action as they threw Jonah into the sea.

"It is better to be in the sea than to be in Ninevah", Jonah might have thought. He would have preferred to die than to see those wretched people escape God's punishment. As he was thinking this he saw the huge whale approaching him with its wide-open mouth. Jonah did not realize that God was giving him another opportunity to change his narrow-minded attitude. As minutes ran into hours, and hours to days, Jonah began to pray for deliverance.

Having been spewed up on the shore by the whale, Jonah knew that it was useless to run away from God. The popular words of King and Psalmist David, "Where can I hide from your Spirit…. If I ascend to the heavens, you are there; if I lie down in Sheol, you are there too" (Ps 139:7-12), might have resonated in his heart. Realizing that it was futile to ignore God's commands, he reluctantly succumbed to God's will.

When God commanded a second time, he decided to go and obey it anyway. He made several short cuts and announced to the people in a condescending and judgmental fashion, "Forty days more and Nineveh shall be destroyed" (Jon 3: 4). There was no message for conversion or repentance. Strangely, Jonah did not want the people to believe his words and amend their ways. He wanted his mission to be a failure!

He was horrified to see the change in the attitude of the people, beginning with the greatest to the least. They wanted to repent and convert! That was not what Jonah hoped. Still Jonah thought, "They are so wicked, God will surely destroy them in forty days. My words will come to pass". He waited in anticipation to see the destruction of these wicked people. He could not understand why God would show mercy to the Gentiles. He complained to God, "This is why I fled at first to Tarshish. I knew that you are a gracious and merciful God, slow to anger, rich in clemency, loathe to punish" (Jon 4: 2). He was too angry and disgusted to respond when God asked him, "Have you any reason to be angry?" (Jon 4:4)

Jonah did not want to understand God's graciousness and mercy. He felt that the only people who deserved God's favor were the chosen ones, who acknowledged the living God and obeyed His commands. Those who worshiped foreign gods and led lives contrary to God's commandments were to be destroyed. He could not understand how God could grant forgiveness to those who had done abominable things. He truly felt that his anger was justifiable and God's mercy extremely unrealistic.

Hoping against hope, Jonah waited in the hot sun at the outskirts of the city to see its destruction. When the tree grew fast and provided him shade, Jonah was happy. When it withered the next day, he became furious. He did not understand that God was teaching him a valid lesson. The conversation that took place between Jonah and God was quite hilarious. Jonah was like a child, pouting when things did not turn out according to his whims. God patiently told him, "You seemed to be concerned over a plant that cost you no labor, so how much more should I be concerned over whole hosts of peoples and other living beings in Ninevah?" (Jon 4:10-11) Jonah must have gasped in disbelief when God said, "they too are my children."

The same love of God, incarnate in the person of Jesus, would challenge the narrow-mindedness of some of his listeners. He would invite them to go beyond their pettiness and self- centeredness. Simon the Pharisee represented all who thought of God's favor as restricted only for the chosen perfect ones (Lk 7: 36-49). Jesus would constantly remind his listeners that God is the God of the second chance, who constantly invites all people to enter into a loving relationship with Him. Jesus was critical of those who exhibited self-righteousness and smugness. God's patient love is revealed in the words of Jesus, "I have not come to call the righteous, but sinners to repentance" (Lk 5:31).

It is so easy to pronounce judgment on others and blame them for their misgivings. At times, the human heart might even rejoice at the calamities others face, especially if they belong to a rival family, tribe, nation or even religion. The God of love does not want us to rejoice in the pain and sufferings of others, but requires us to pray and help to alleviate the pain and suffering of others.

"Anyone who has truly experienced God's mercy and goodness would wish for all to experience them." – author.

JOB: Even the Righteous Suffer greatly

"Where were you when I founded the earth? Tell me if you have understanding. Who determined its size? Who stretched out the measuring line for it?" (Job 38:4-5)

One of the most difficult questions ever posed is "why should good and innocent people suffer?" No satisfactory answer is readily forthcoming. The closest answer could be found in the life of Job, but still the answer remains vague at best. Ultimately one is challenged to realize how small one is in comparison to the mysteries of God.

Job constantly said "yes" to God and "no" to evil. His piety and devotion were well known to all. Every aspect of his life was determined by his relationship with God. He loved God above all things and never questioned Him even when things did not go according to his plans. Like everyone, there were ups and downs, and twists and turns in his life. But he never allowed any of those to affect his relationship with God, his family and his neighbors. He always said, "My blessings are too numerous for me to fret over the little struggles of life". Indeed, God had blessed Job abundantly.

While Job was busy with his routine activities, there was an interesting development in the heavens that included Job without his knowledge. God was speaking so proudly of His servant Job. But the adversary, Satan, very interestingly countered, "true, when things go well, it is easy to lead· a good and upright life". He challenged God to change the fortunes of Job and see how he would fare in moments of crisis. God allowed Satan to have control over Job by inflicting adversities, but never causing any harm to his life.

In one day, there was a complete reversal of Job's fortunes. Four messengers brought Job news of the complete ruin of his servants, all his animals, all his possessions and – the most painful of all – the death of all his ten children. One day he was blessed with ten children, and enjoyed many possessions, servants, immense wealth and a happy life. And the next day he found himself childless, poor and destitute. Job could have had every reason to be angry and question God for these unexpected calamities in his life. Rather, he uttered these incredible words to express his absolute dependence on God, "Naked I came forth from my mother's womb, and naked I shall go back again. The Lord gave and the Lord has taken away; blessed be the name of the Lord" (Job 1:21).

As Job remained innocent and uncomplaining after losing all his possessions and posterity, Satan suggested that Job had not been fully tried and tested yet. God granted Satan another permission to afflict sufferings on Job's body, but spare his life. Job's body was covered with severe boils from the soles of his feet to the crown of his head. Overwhelmed by agony and frustration, Job's wife went on to suggest, "Curse God and die" (Job 2:9). Job held on to his conviction that all things came from God as gifts, at times in the form of good, and at times in the form of evil. God had not caused any evil upon Job; rather it was the work of Satan. Job, who thought everything came from God seemed to resolve his conviction that even the sufferings in his life were somehow part of God's plan.

The three friends of Job — Eliphaz, Bildad and Zophar — came to be with Job to offer him their sympathy and support. For seven days and seven nights they silently sat with Job. None of them were ready to talk. They were trying to make sense of the unexpected tragedies that had happened to Job. Job's pain was great and his troubles numerous. As hours turned to days, his pain became too intolerable. Job, finally overwhelmed by his suffering, opened his mouth and cursed the day he was born. This initiated a conversation that probed into the reasons for Job's suffering. In trying to make sense of the situation, Job's friends suggested that he was either impatient, or may have committed evil, and probably deserved greater punishment than he was experiencing.

Eliphaz told Job that he had attempted to comfort many. According to Eliphaz, misfortunes had affected Job's patience and it seemed clear that Job never understood the pain of others when he offered them his advice. Eliphaz also believed that Job might have committed some serious sin to offend God. Bildad thought the reason for all Job's calamities might have been Job's children. Zophar implied that whatever be the wickedness that Job had committed, the punishment seemed insufficient. Job increasingly began losing patience with his friends and grew irritated. They were fine when they were quiet. He asked them to be silent rather than giving him false remedies and telling lies.

Job looked for vindication from God. He searched for God to reason with Him, but could not see God physically. Job also admitted that he did not even understand himself well enough to plead his case to God effectively. Hearing this, his friends then categorically said that Job lacked appropriate fear of God. A fourth friend Elihu stated that Job seemed to spend too much time vindicating himself instead of God. He also assumed the wickedness of Job as the reason for his suffering.

When God finally interrupted, He did not give logical answers to the questions concerning Job's suffering. Rather, He patiently tried to teach Job by inviting him to broaden his understanding rather than foolishly believe that he could find all the answers. He asked Job questions about the details of creation. Job only humbly acknowledged God's unlimited power and the limitations of human knowledge. Job's friends were seeking to find justification for Job's suffering but it was beyond their comprehension. Job, on the other hand, admitted his limitations and renewed his trust in the Lord. Job's family and possessions were restored and his later days were more blessed than the earlier ones.

There are no satisfactory answers to the questions, "why should good and innocent people suffer?" or "why does an all powerful-God allow good people to suffer?" The story of Job does make it clear that God does not cause suffering. It is rather the work of the devil to turn people against God. One might not be able to find justifiable answers for the causes of one's pain. One may never understand. Job had to humbly realize his human limitations and accept the mysteries of God's ways. Ultimately, Job surrendered himself totally to God.

Unexpected sufferings and moments of crisis may cause a person to ask this question: "Where is God?" A parent who is faced with the untimely death of his/her only child may cry out to God with this same question. Could God answer, "I AM at the same place when they crucified my only child"?

From the cross on Calvary a cry was heard, "My God, my God, why have you abandoned me?" Some time later, from the same cross these determined words were heard, "Father into your hands I commend my spirit".

"He tells us to trust Him enough to believe He knows what he is doing. When His actions don't make sense, trust Him..... When the bottom falls out and life turns hard, trust Him. Good times and bad, happy and sad, trust Him. When I try to explain Him away or reduce Him to neat little formulas, I show a lack of faith, not a wealth of it" – Mark Tabb *Out of the Whirlwind.*

ELIJAH: Prophet Par Excellence

"This is enough, O Lord! Take my life, for I am no better than my fathers. He lay down to sleep... an angel touched him and ordered him to get up and eat" (1 Kg 19:4-5).

Ahab was one of the worst kings of Israel: "Ahab, son of Omri, did evil in the sight of the Lord more than any of his predecessors" (1 Kg 16:30). His sin surpassed all others as he went on to marry the Sidonian princess Jezebel, erected an altar to Baal in the very temple that he had built in honor of Baal in Samaria. He went on to commit the abominable sin of idolatry as he worshiped Baal with his wife.

God sent the best to counter the worst. From the beginning, Elijah's heart was with God. He avoided everything that was evil and devoted his life solely to God. He was so zealous for God and courageously proclaimed His word to Ahab the King, "As the Lord, the God of Israel lives, whom I serve, during these years there shall be no dew or rain except at my word" (1 Kg 17:1). Ahab, whose heart was totally closed to God, might have laughed along with Jezebel and her prophets at Elijah and ordered him to leave his kingdom. God's powerful word, spoken through Elijah, was fulfilled as the whole kingdom was stricken with famine. When famine advanced, God touched the heart of the widow of Zarephath who provided for Elijah. Her little provision of flour and oil never exhausted!

In the third year of the famine, God asked Elijah to go back to Ahab. Famine had severely affected Samaria. It had become a national disaster. People were greatly suffering on account of the abominable acts of the king, the queen, and her prophets. Queen Jezebel, the wife of Ahab, had accused the prophets and all who feared Yahweh as the reason for the famine. She was enraged and killed the prophets of the Lord who refused to worship Baal. The countless prophets of Baal who lived comfortably at the expense of Jezebel were always encouraging her to put to death all who worshiped Yahweh.

When Ahab saw Elijah, he was outraged and called him a disturber of Israel. Elijah stood his ground boldly and proclaimed that it was the king and his family who were disturbing Israel by forsaking the living God and His commands and by worshiping Baal. He challenged the prophets of Baal, who were four hundred and fifty in number at Mount Carmel to offer an acceptable sacrifice to Baal. It was a contest between Elijah, the true prophet of the living God, and hundreds of false prophets of Baal. It was going to be a moment of truth for all to see. The prophets of Baal prepared the sacrifice and called upon their deity to accept the offering. When there was total silence even after mutilating themselves, Elijah mocked them and suggested "Call louder, for he is a god and may be meditating, or may have retired or may be on a journey. Perhaps he is asleep and must be awakened" (1 Kg 18 27).

As hours passed and when Baal's prophets seemed exhausted and exasperated, Elijah began to set up the altar before all the people. Drenching the altar and the offering with water, Elijah called upon the name of the living God. The fire of the Lord consumed the sacrifice and manifested His greatness before all the people. Elijah was consumed with zeal for the Lord and he caught hold of all the prophets of Baal and slew them.

The victory seemed to be short-lived, as the whole affair had outraged Jezebel. The humiliated woman sought the life of Elijah. Her fierce anger intimidated Elijah and he escaped from her grasp. In the desert he asked the Lord to take his life. He was so discouraged by the turn of events and the uncertainty of his life. He felt that his mission was an utter failure. How could the great prophet of God, who had seen God's awesome power, succumb to fear and desperation? We might wonder. He could possibly have been affected by his constant struggle for truth, the continuous rejection of the people, the threat of the evil enemy, and his own feelings of failure. Through him God had provided every possible sign required for the conversion of the king, the queen, and the people. Elijah was heartbroken at seeing the uncertainty of Ahab and the vengeance of Jezebel. For a moment he allowed doubts to seep through his being and wanted to give up. His desperation was so great that he wanted to give up and die. The angel of the Lord assured him of God's protection and told him to get up and eat for the long journey ahead. After forty days he reached Horeb.

At the very mountain where the people of Israel received the Ten Commandments, Elijah was assured of God's protection. He witnessed the powerful experiences of violent forms of nature in the form of a mighty wind, earthquakes and fire. But, alas, God was not present in any of them. Then there was the tiny whispering sound and when Elijah heard it, he had to cover his face in his cloak and went and stood at the entrance of the cave. Through these events, God was telling Elijah that while He manifests His awesome power in stupendous acts of nature, He is not in nature. He accomplishes His purpose through his gentle voice, the voice of truth. The marvelous acts of nature might get people's attention, but what truly leads them to repentance and a change of heart is the message of truth, which is like a small voice always present, but often neglected. The message of truth has always been there. And all the prophets of God are to proclaim it through their lives as Elijah did. He was instructed to anoint new kings for the people and to anoint Elisha as the prophet to succeed him.

The best — Elijah — visited the worst — Ahab for the last time. Ahab had coveted the vineyard of Naboth, who had refused to part with his ancestral property. Jezebel, the wicked queen took the matter into her own hands and through treachery had Naboth killed and took possession of the vineyard. Elijah uttered the words of doom to Ahab that all of his household would be killed, and Ahab's blood would be licked by the dogs and Jezebel would be eaten by dogs at the wall of Jezreel. They had brought this punishment upon themselves by their evil deeds. Having completed his work and after having anointed the young Elisha to succeed him, Elijah was taken up to heaven in a flaming chariot. In the Jewish mind, he was expected to return before the arrival of the Messiah.

The zealous Elijah always carried on the work of the Lord. There were moments when natural human fear and doubts took control over him. However, he remained faithful to the end. This greatest prophet is mentioned several times in the New Testament. In the gospels, he is likened to John the Baptist, the herald of the Messiah. "He (John) will go before him in the spirit and power of Elijah to turn the hearts of fathers towards their children and the disobedient to the understanding of the righteous, to prepare a people fit for the Lord" (Lk 1:17). Elijah would be seen with Moses, conversing with Jesus at the moment of His transfiguration, where He revealed His glory and when the Father confirmed His Son's mission (Mk 9:4).

"Expecting the world to treat you fairly because you are a good person is a little like expecting the bull not to attack you because you are a vegetarian." – *Dennis Wholey*

JEZEBEL: Manipulation Exemplified!

"When Jezebel learned that Naboth had been stoned to death, she said to Ahab, "Go on, take possession of the vineyard of Naboth the Jezerite which he refused to sell you, because he is not alive, but dead" (1 Kg 21:15).

If Ruth is admired for her filial piety and devotion, Jezebel is frowned upon for her wickedness and evil ways. Both were Gentile women. One is remembered for embracing the truth, and the other for constantly trying to destroy it.

Ahab the worst king of Israel married Jezebel the daughter of Ethbaal, the king of the Sidonians. Ahab was already wicked, however, Jezebel contributed her share in making him the most infamous king who ever ruled over Israel. As her father was both king and priest of Baal, she was initiated into the cult practices at an early age. She embraced it enthusiastically as it appealed to her sensuality and gave her a sense of power.

Like many surrounding cultures, the worship of Baal involved activities of sensual natures and sexual pleasures. Temple prostitution was commonly practiced as part of their religious ceremonies. Activities of a sexual nature played a significant role in their fertility cults. She had the power of being a princess and her best asset was her beauty. Her charm gave her an advantage in winning over the hearts of many powerful men. She was not only beautiful but also possessed a cunning personality. She had realized early on that physical beauty had a depreciating value, but power gives control. She set out to gain control of everything.

The marriage between the Israelite king Ahab and the Sidonian princess Jezebel created a new alliance between the two nations. For Jezebel, this was the best opportunity to introduce her culture and religion to her newly found home. She had always regarded Yahweh, the God of Israel, as her enemy. She believed Baal to be the true god and wanted to destroy every other alleged supernatural power in existence. She gained Ahab's confidence by her charm and when she suggested building a temple for Baal, he did not object. After constructing the temple, she had him erect an altar for Baal, and eventually led him to denounce Yahweh by worshiping Baal. She convinced him of Baal's mighty power and ridiculed the God of the Israelites. She won over the trust of the vast majority of people in Israel through her charm and sensual cult practices that led them away from God. She also unleashed persecution and death upon those who remained faithful to Yahweh. She was set to destroy faith in Yahweh either by her seduction or through persecution.

She met her rival, Elijah, who presented himself to be the prophet of the God of Israel. The moment she saw him, she flinched and wanted to destroy him by all means. She laughed at the words Elijah spoke to Ahab, "During these years there shall be no dew or rain except at my word" (I Kg 17:2). She told Ahab that their god Baal could discredit the words of Elijah and make everyone believe that he is the true god. She boasted that Baal had supreme power over rain and storm. She consulted Baal's prophets and they assured her imminent rain and prosperity in place of drought and famine. But as months rolled into years with no signs of rain and increased famine, they convinced her that Baal was angry because of those who worshipped Yahweh. She believed that unless and until she killed Elijah and all the prophets of Yahweh, Baal would not be appeased. She went on a rampage and began killing all the prophets of the Lord. As she could not find Elijah, she concluded that he must be dead. "There was no way he could survive this severe famine," she thought.

She was greatly surprised to hear that Elijah was alive and looking healthy even after three years of famine. He presented himself to challenge her to see whose god was the true God – Yahweh or Baal. Jezebel had no doubt Baal would strike down Elijah and establish his superior power. As the events unfolded, Elijah won the contest, as God revealed His overwhelming power. Jezebel was horrified to hear that Baal did not answer the petitions of his prophets. She was outraged to hear of the slaughter of all the prophets of Baal with whom she had committed many abominable sins.

She was equally annoyed at seeing Ahab exhibiting traits of remorse and a desire to go back to Yahweh. Ahab had witnessed the power of God and the defeat of Baal and his prophets. He knew that it was the power of God that had brought rain upon the earth after three years of famine. But Jezebel had such a firm control over Ahab that she did not allow him to dwell on his new realizations. Ahab once again lost the opportunity to correct his ways. She vowed to take revenge on Elijah and had him on the run. She diligently searched for him to have him killed. She convinced Ahab that killing Elijah would demonstrate the power of Baal and usher in a new age of peace and prosperity.

Her control over Ahab and her manipulative powers were best portrayed in the episode of Naboth. Ahab had coveted the vineyard of Naboth that was next to his palace. Although Ahab promised to exchange it with another vineyard or pay him money for it, Naboth refused to part with his ancestral property. Naboth was a God-fearing man who valued the long-standing tradition that inherited property should not be sold to anyone outside the family. When Ahab heard of Naboth's decision, he was both angry and depressed. For Jezebel, this was the best opportunity to both demonstrate her loyalty to her husband and to prove her power. She had enjoyed unlimited power at her palace and she could not stand anyone objecting to the desire of the king.

Though she did not believe or observe any of the religious laws of Israel, she knew them well. She knew that the testimony of two witnesses would be sufficient to condemn someone to death (Dt 17:6). She forged a letter with Ahab's name and seal and sent it to the elders and nobles, whom she had brought under her manipulative control. The letter stated: "Proclaim a fast and set Naboth at the head of the people. Next, get two scoundrels to face him and accuse him of having cursed God and the king. Then take him out and stone him to death" (1 Kg 21:9-10). With a cold-blooded nature, she executed her plan and had Naboth killed. She felt triumphant at her achievement and informed Ahab of his newly acquired possession. The fact of Naboth's innocence or commitment to ancestral law meant nothing to her.

The cry of the innocent reaches to the heavens. God instructed Elijah to confront Ahab and Jezebel for the last time. All of God's signs and warnings had been completely rejected by this cruel and vicious couple. Ultimately their evil deeds would catch up with them, and Elijah at God's promptings proclaimed their impending deaths.

The "spirit of Jezebel" would continue to hound the true believers. In the New Testament she is portrayed as the false prophetess, who seeks to mislead the people from true faith: "You tolerate the woman Jezebel, who calls herself a prophetess, who teaches and misleads my servants to play the harlot and to eat food sacrificed to idols" (Rev 3: 20). God's people are constantly challenged to embrace and live by the truth.

When one lives the life of a lie, there is no sense of fairness or justice. In place of honesty, manipulation and deception reign over one's heart, and determine one's actions. Such a person often views those who live honest and godly lives are often viewed as his/her enemies. The faster a person realizes the fact that the true enemy is within oneself, the sooner will be the possibility of escape from the pitiful state of lies and deception.

"Deception is a cruel act. It often has many players on different stages that corrode the soul" – Donna A. Favors.

JEREMIAH:
The Struggle of a True Prophet

"The days are coming, says the Lord, when I will make a new covenant with the house of Israel and the house of Judah.... I will place my law within them, and write it upon their hearts; I will be their God and they shall be my people" (Jer 31: 31-33).

No true prophet had a smooth ride when he took his call seriously. Jeremiah, whose prophetic activities lasted for over a period of four decades, took his mission to heart and had to endure severe heartaches and pain. But he persisted, always being faithful to the living God. Continuing on the legacy of all his predecessors, he preached on important themes of true piety, social justice, absolute loyalty to the one true God, individual responsibility, repentance and conversion. Like a true prophet, he upheld truth and criticized all who sided with falsehood. He was constantly targeted for his unpopular messages, which often challenged the way the kings, priests, false prophets and many of the people lived.

The call of Jeremiah revealed God's plan for the young man. He was surprised to hear the powerful words of God: "Before I formed you in the womb, I knew you. Before you were born I dedicated you, a prophet to the nations I appointed you" (Jer1:5). Though Jeremiah protested, citing personal inadequacies and his young age for such a gigantic task, God assured him that he was the right person. Jeremiah seemed to have no choice but to accept the challenge. It was as if God was telling Jeremiah, "I do not call the qualified, but rather qualify those whom I call". God had set Jeremiah apart for a mission that only he could fulfill. He was commissioned to "uproot and tear down; destroy and to demolish; to build and to plant" (Jer 1:10). It was a mission that involved radical change and new beginnings.

The changing world events of the time demanded the presence of a person who would not run away when he faced great challenges. The Assyrians, Egyptians and Babylonians were all constantly trying to overpower the chosen people. The leaders of the chosen people were corrupt, causing people to forget the living God and embrace the worship of foreign gods. In the midst of this chaos, there existed a pressing need to bring people back to God. Jeremiah had a tough task at hand! God assured him of His constant presence and protection. Jeremiah's call in some ways was symbolic of what God has in store for every person. How comforting and strengthening it would be if every person acknowledged that God knew and called each one even before a person is formed in the womb!

Jeremiah had wholeheartedly supported the religious reforms initiated by King Josiah, who had tried to implement many steps to bring people back to God. Both Josiah and Jeremiah believed that the dismal plight of the people was caused by their own infidelity to God's Covenant. Josiah had come to power at a time of extreme religious corruption, which had led to many forms of idolatry. He also had initiated a restoration of the temple and believed that if people turned away from their wicked ways, God would not carry out His threat of destruction. King Josiah truly enjoyed the support of Jeremiah whose message always entailed repentance and conversion. Unfortunately, Josiah was unable to complete the reforms as he was killed in a battle with the Egyptians.

It was a great setback for Jeremiah. He began to witness the corrupt leaders emerging everywhere and leading people astray. Kings, priests, and leaders of the people were wicked in their lives and affairs. He felt that the evil forces were corrupting the leaders and as a result the whole nation was drifting farther and farther from God's ways. Time after time he warned the people against taking for granted the mercy and patience of God. They were constantly testing God with their abominable acts of idolatry and cruel deeds of social injustice on the weak and powerless.

Jeremiah wondered how painful it must have been for God to see His people constantly turning their backs on Him. He also knew that God loved them too much to leave them in their state of destruction. He neither feared for his safety, nor looked for popular acceptance. He knew that his message of truth would make many turn against him. Jeremiah did not mince his words when he addressed the powerful. He challenged the false prophets who avoided the actual situation and preached popular messages of prosperity and success. He chastised them for giving false messages of hope when in reality they were faced with danger from every side.

He had to pay a heavy price for his prophetic activities: he received death threats; he was imprisoned; he was thrown down a well; he was called a traitor; and he experienced rejection and loneliness. In the midst of such agonizing moments Jeremiah struggled with his own awareness of failures and inadequacies. There were times when he struggled with God and felt that God had duped him and he was paying too great a price for his obedience. Still, like a true prophet, he would set aside his personal sufferings and focus on the mission.

He prophesied the destruction of Jerusalem and the temple. But his words fell on deaf ears. When it did come to pass, Jeremiah was left in Jerusalem among the ruins. His heart was aching as he stood by the ruins where the majestic temple once stood. People had witnessed the splendor of God many a time and yet they were lured away to the worship of false gods. Even though God's chosen people were scattered by the Assyrians and Babylonians, Jeremiah knew that God would bring them back and fulfill His promises. He knew that there would be an end to the exile, that the people would return and that the temple would once again be restored. He would remind the people of a loving and forgiving God who in time would unveil better days for them.

He believed that God's act of restoration would lead to the establishment of a New Covenant, written in the hearts of the people. The New Covenant would not be written on the stone tablets, but rather on the hearts of human beings. It would be an act of God and therefore everlasting. It would be made with the house of Israel and the house of Judah, indicating all the people. This would lead to conversion of heart and change of mind for all and result in the forgiveness of sin and inheritance of eternal life.

God would initiate the New Covenant with the people through His Son Jesus. The New Covenant would be established by

Jesus and ratified by his blood. At the Last Supper, Jesus would take the cup, fill it with wine and say, "This cup is the new covenant in my blood, which will be shed for you" (Lk 22:20). The New Covenant involved entering into a life-giving relationship with Christ.

"No sustainable change is possible unless it begins from within as a response to God's invitation and grace" – *author*

ZECHARIAH: Unspeakable Joy

"Immediately his mouth opened, tongue freed and he spoke blessing God" (Lk 1: 64).

God chose a devout, elderly couple to be the parents of the Messenger to announce the arrival of the Messiah. Zechariah and Elizabeth were closer to the grave than to the cradle. Their age would indicate that they were not at a stage in their lives to initiate a new beginning, or take up a new endeavor, or accept a new challenge. Probably the childless couple was resigned to the quiet days of their old age, performing simple tasks in their lives. They could have never imagined the great favor God had in store for them. By choosing the elderly couple, Zechariah and Elizabeth, God proclaimed loud and clear that no limitations of life would be a barrier from accomplishing His purpose.

Zechariah's life centered around God and the Temple. He thanked God daily for the privilege of being a priest. It was his birthright as he was from the priestly family of Aaron. There were thousands of priests and many a time the majority of them had no noticeable function in the Temple. Zechariah had realized early in his life that leading a holy and blameless life before God and the people was the greatest responsibility of a priest. He considered himself fortunate to be married to Elizabeth, who was also descended from a priestly family. They complemented each other well and devoted their lives to God by living a virtuous life.

The reconstruction of the Temple had brought new hope for the people. There was an air of expectation that something great was about to happen. Many were claiming that God was going to fulfill His promises and the Messiah was going to appear immediately. Based on their worldview they also knew that Elijah, Jeremiah or one of the prophets would come announcing the arrival of the Messiah and preparing the hearts of the people. Zechariah and Elizabeth prayed daily to have the grace to see the herald who would help them prepare for the Messiah.

Although they lived a virtuous and holy life, they were affected by the sad reality of childlessness. They hoped and prayed to have children, but with each passing year, they came to the realization that they were not so fortunate as to receive this special gift. It was indeed a painful struggle. Childlessness was frowned upon and was viewed as a matter of shame. It was valid grounds for divorce. A Jew who had a barren wife was presumed to be excluded from God's favor. However, this painful reality or any popular worldview did not diminish their love for one another. Zechariah constantly comforted Elizabeth and asked her to look beyond their deprivation, and to focus on the numerous blessings God had bestowed on them.

Serving as a priest gave Zechariah such great joy that in the temple he forgot about his personal and family trials and focused his attention totally on God. As was the custom, every day one priest was chosen by lot to enter the sanctuary of the Lord to burn incense before the sacrifice was offered. This task was the highlight of a priest's life and in most cases a once-in-a-lifetime privilege. Zechariah was overjoyed for being chosen by lot that day. He felt unworthy to stand in the sanctuary of the Lord and perform the beautiful priestly duty.

Suddenly Zechariah experienced the presence of someone by the altar and thought that he was dreaming. Standing there was an angel, who calmed the fear of Zechariah by these words, "Do not be afraid, Zechariah, because your prayer has been heard" (Lk 1:13a). As he was offering a number of intentions that were in his heart, he was not sure of the specific one the angel was alluding to. Certainly he was not ready to hear the unexpected words from the Angel: "Your wife Elizabeth will bear a son and you shall name him John" (Lk 1:13b). The angel announced further that the child would be filled with the Holy Spirit, serve in the spirit and power of Elijah, and would prepare the way for the Lord.

Zechariah must have been startled at these words. As he knew the Scriptures well, Zechariah was aware of the coming of the herald before the Messiah. Being a practical person, Zechariah could not refrain from making his doubts known about the impossibility of the whole situation, particularly due to the age of the couple. Even the words of the Angel, that he would be mute until the events happened, did not take away the awesome feelings Zechariah had in his heart. He came out mute, unable to utter a word, and people realized that something special had happened to him in the sanctuary.

"How will I communicate this wonderful news to my wife?" Zechariah might have wondered. The moment he arrived at his house and saw that glow on Elizabeth's face, he knew there was no need for any words. They sat in silence for a very long time, holding hands, looking at each other and seeing the miraculous presence of God in one another. Their silence communicated in a way more than any number of words could convey. God had heard their prayer and answered in ways more than they ever expected.

Time after time Zechariah thought about the beautiful experience, savoring it in his heart. He felt humbled at the thought of God sending His angel to reveal His plan of salvation. Whenever he thought of his doubting words to the angel, he grimaced with shame and guilt. The words of doubt were a spontaneous reaction to a very unlikely favor. He did not consider his muteness as any form of punishment, because he thought he deserved worse for doubting God's words. As time went on he might have felt his muteness as a blessing so he could recollect and cherish his amazing experience of God.

His joy was indescribable as he held his newborn boy in his arms. There were many reasons for great joy: having a child in their old age, the removal of the shame of childlessness, and having a boy to carry on the family legacy, providing safety and security for their old age. However, the cause of Zechariah's greatest joy was the realization that God had set this little boy apart for a special purpose – to be the Herald of the Messiah!

When the time came to name the child, Elizabeth volunteered information, but all seemed to doubt her. As he wrote down the name 'John' on the tablet, he felt the touch of God on his lips. He opened his mouth and sang the marvelous praise of God. His words truly reflected confidence in God's promises and a solemn proclamation of God's powerful deeds for the salvation of the world. In the most beautiful way he recalled

God's glorious achievements in the past, and God's plans for the future. Looking at the tiny face of John, Zechariah spoke with great pride and joy the incredible task his son was to fulfill – prepare the way of the Messiah by preaching the message of repentance and conversion.

"If you have prayed for rain, go out with an umbrella" - author

ELIZABETH:
Never too Late to Receive a Blessing.

"So has the Lord done for me at time when He has seen fit to take away my disgrace before others" (Lk 1:25).

There are several women in the Bible whose experiences of pain and shame on account of barrenness have become decisive moments of God's comforting actions. Elizabeth stands in the long line of witnesses upon whom God's favor rested in a way that was beyond her expectations. Her ceaseless prayers were answered with a son, whose identity and mission would never be forgotten in history.

Elizabeth was born in the respectable priestly family of Aaron. As she grew up in an environment of faith and religious practices, she developed a great devotion to God at an early age. Her marriage to Zechariah, a respectable man from the priestly division of Abijah deepened her commitment to God. Both were godly and observed God's commandments faithfully. They were righteous before God and people and led blameless lives.

As months rolled into years, the devout couple began to grieve over the fact of childlessness. They prayed fervently to God to bless their lives with a child. In their culture there were always speculations as to why a woman was barren. It was normally attributed to some sin, either of the couple or of their ancestors. Sometimes it was attributed to some form of demonic oppression. On a social level it was a grave matter of shame. For a woman, it was a cause of instability and insecurity in family life as childlessness was viewed as legitimate grounds for divorce.

There must have been moments when Elizabeth stood in sadness, watching mothers pass by with their tiny children. Every time she held a little child in her arms she must have experienced pangs of sorrow with regard to her condition. The laughter or cry of an infant might have brought tears to her eyes, trickling down onto her cheeks. There must have been people who said cruel things behind her back. She faced all these realities with patience and grace. None of these experiences ever lessened her devotion to God. She trusted and believed that God knew what was best for her and Zechariah. She must have thanked God daily for Zechariah who exhibited a tremendous sense of patience and understanding. She was able to perceive his tremendous pain beyond his calming assurance and comforting words. This awareness only made her more determined to knock at the doors of heaven with complete trust and faith.

On the day Zechariah was chosen to offer incense at the temple something special happened to her. She felt a sense of peace, calmness and joy enveloping her. She experienced an energy and enthusiasm that she had not felt in years. When Zechariah returned, she found his face radiating with joy and hope. Though he was mute and unable to speak, she knew something extraordinary was about to happen. As they sat in perfect silence, the moments of stillness communicated volumes more than any number of words.

As days passed by, she realized that God's favor was upon her and that she had become pregnant. For the first few months, she went into seclusion. Her words were powerful, "The Lord has done for me at a time when He has seen fit to take away my disgrace before others (Lk 1:25). She acknowledged God's timely favor that dispelled any disgrace associated with being a barren woman. God was acting at a time when she least expected and His deeds outdid her hopes and dreams.

More good news was to follow with the arrival of her young cousin, Mary. There had been no news from Mary's family for a while, except that of Mary's proposed marriage to Joseph in the near future. Elizabeth was overjoyed at seeing Mary. However, when Mary greeted Elizabeth, something beautiful happened. The infant in her womb leaped as if to acknowledge the presence of the Savior. Elizabeth was filled with the Holy Spirit and cried out "blessed are you among women, and blessed is the fruit of your womb" (Lk 1: 42). It was as if Elizabeth knew right away that the child in Mary's womb was the most Blessed One, who would alter the history of the world, and redeem and transform the destiny of the human race.

Two simple women found great favor in God's sight! They recognized the impossible happening in their lives and acknowledged it with great joy. On a human level it was impossible for Elizabeth to conceive in her old age. Similarly, for Mary being a virgin, it was impossible for her to be with child. But both women, by their experiences, proclaimed loud and clear that "with God all things are possible".

It must have been a difficult pregnancy for Elizabeth. But nothing took away the joy of her experience. She cherished each and every movement of her child growing within her. Sometimes, she felt, he was too eager to begin his mission. He had already acknowledged the presence of the Savior when Mary visited them. Zechariah, still mute, was always at her side with a serene expression on his face. She must have cried with joy at seeing the tender face of her newborn baby. This was probably the most cherished moment of her entire life. Right before her eyes she was witnessing God's favor at a very unlikely time. Never did she doubt God's might and power.

When it was time to name the baby, she made it clear to them that he would be called John. Everyone objected, saying there was no such name among their kinfolks. It was unlikely for a woman to be so bold in public. Elizabeth, having known the decision from God through Zachariah stood her ground. When they gave Zechariah the tablet and he wrote on it 'John', all were amazed. More surprises followed when suddenly he spoke after nine months of silence. His words were of great praise to God who had done marvelous things in their midst.

Elizabeth is a towering example of perseverance and persistence. Life is often not fair and when there are unwarranted sufferings and pain, faithfulness to God keeps one grounded and prayer opens the doors of possibilities. Elizabeth proclaims loud and clear, "never give up or give in. It is better to be late to receive a blessing than never at all".

Elizabeth's words are immortalized as a beautiful Christian prayer: "Hail Mary". Its inspiration is found in the infancy narratives in the Gospel of Luke. When Mary visited Elizabeth, out of joy Elizabeth says, "Most blessed are you among women, and blessed is the fruit of your womb" (Lk 1:42). The words of this simple woman, Elizabeth, have become a powerful form of prayer as it leads us to the fruit of Mary's womb – Jesus.

"Don't pray when it rains if you don't pray when the sun shines" – Satchel Paige

JOHN THE BAPTIST:
Courageous Messenger

"In those days John the Baptist appeared, preaching in the desert of Judea, and saying, 'Repent, for the kingdom of heaven is at hand!"' (Mt 3:12).

John's was a singular mission: prepare the people for the arrival of the Messiah. He challenged the people to turn away from sin and embrace the way of the Lord. In his short life he pointed everyone in the direction of the Savior and lived out his bold statement "He must increase and I must decrease". He was an embodiment of courage and always embraced truth, even when it meant persecution and death.

Everyone looked at him with a sense of awe and wonder. Many times as a child, John had heard people say that he was special and destined for greatness. His aging parents, Zechariah and Elizabeth, made several references to the visits of the angels and the special task at hand for him. He heard about his father's encounter with the angel, his subsequent state of muteness, and how his tongue was freed when he wrote 'John' at the naming ceremony. His parents had lovingly conveyed to him the good news that the time was at hand for the arrival of the Messiah. As a child, he did not fully understand what they meant when they indicated that it was going to be his responsibility to prepare the people for the coming of the Messiah and to announce the arrival of God's kingdom.

From the beginning he loved to live a simple life. He did not crave any possessions. There was a burning desire in his heart to please God always by obeying his statutes and decrees. Even before he understood what it meant to take a Nazirite vow he was living it out. The reality that he lost his parents at a young age made him search for a quiet life, and to discern what God had in store for him. It was natural to grieve over the death of his beloved parents. However, the fire burning within made him forget about the personal loss and focus on his mission.

Preparing the way for the Messiah was no easy task. There were all kinds of stories that were floating around: some hoped for grand social and structural changes; some imagined that it would be similar to a military conquest; some believed that all the wicked and evil people would be destroyed; some were talking about great prosperity and peace in the land; and some were claiming that the world would be instantly perfect at the arrival of the Messiah.

John knew that the Messiah transcended all those expectations. He knew the best preparation for the arrival of the Messiah should begin from within oneself. All other changes would automatically follow if there occurred a change of mind and heart. A new mind and new heart were possible only when there was repentance and conversion.

He burst forth onto the scene with this message of repentance. His fiery words attracted many people and they were turning to him in response. Tax collectors, prostitutes and other public offenders were coming to him in great numbers. Deep within, John knew that all people stood in need of God's mercy. His anger blazed when he saw the self-righteous religious leaders who evaded such a move as if to portray perfect holiness before everyone. He knew that beyond their pristine physical appearance, they were rotten inside. They seemed to succeed in hiding their real sinful nature from everyone. But John believed that they could not hide anything from God. Hence he challenged them with words that made them look deep within. In the process of issuing a call to repentance and renewal, he had made several enemies, but he did not seem to care.

There were always people who were inquiring if he was the Messiah. He felt absolutely humbled and he made it clear that he was not worthy to untie the Messiah's sandals. The Messiah was holiness incarnate in whom there was no blemish. He was like a spotless lamb, the Lamb of God who would take away the sin of the world.

There were many who were attracted by his life and his message and wanted to be his disciples. John talked the talk and walked the walk. People marveled at his austere life and the simplicity he manifested. However, it was his radical message that demanded turning away from sin and turning to God with a humble heart that attracted many. All who followed John hoped for better days ahead, but John knew his mission was to be fulfilled in the near future.

He made it very clear to them that he was only a messenger for the promised Messiah. His task was to get everyone ready for God's decisive action in history that would manifest His plan for human beings. "I must decrease and he must increase," he constantly told them. He reminded them that his baptism was only one of repentance, but the baptism that would be brought by the Messiah was going to be in the Holy Spirit and Fire. The baptism of the Messiah would initiate a radical break from the sinful past, and commence a new beginning which would lead all to be reconciled with God.

John had heard of his cousin Jesus from his parents before they died. There was always a sense of mystery surrounding him and the stories about him. John's mother had assured him that he knew the Messiah even before he was born. "Would I recognize him? Would he be the promised Messiah?" John wondered.

Then one day John saw him. Jesus was coming towards him, where John was baptizing. Jesus was soon standing before John in waist deep water as if ready for baptism. Time must have stood still when the two looked at each other. There was such a great calming effect that radiated from Jesus. There was no doubt in John's mind as to who was standing before him. This was the moment for which he had been sent, the fulfillment of his mission. All that John could utter was "I must be baptized by you." Looking intently at John, Jesus replied, "Allow it now, for thus it is fitting for us to fulfill all righteousness" (Mt 3:15). Then Jesus bowed his head and lowered himself before John into the water. John needed no confirmation, yet his heart was thrilled when he heard the voice from heaven, "This is my beloved son, in whom I am well pleased." The gushing sound of the wind and the mighty presence of the spirit assured John that he had completed his task and it was time to move on and to leave the scene.

John's final act was to bear witness to the message of truth. He had courageously challenged King Herod about his immoral life with his brother's wife, Herodias. The outraged and conniving sinful woman saw John as a threat and plotted to execute him.

Though John's ministry was brief, the effect of his ministry had been great. His singular mission was to point everyone to the direction of the Savior. Our life will become more meaningful when we can be a true sign, pointing others towards the Savior of the world.

"Truth is not only violated by falsehood; it may be equally outraged by silence" - Henry Frederic Amiel

JOSEPH: A Just Man

"Joseph, her husband, since he was a righteous man, yet unwilling to expose her to shame, decided to divorce her quietly" (Mt 1:19).

If you, as a father, have a situation where you should let your child be under the guardianship of another man, it is only natural that you will inquire diligently about that person. You would not make a hasty decision. But if you are so fortunate as to have the option of choosing any man from the whole world, you would naturally look for the best-qualified person. Of course your sense of qualifications would depend on your priorities. God was faced with that option and His gaze fell upon Joseph of the house of David. He was a just man and a hardworking carpenter. Once he became aware of God's plan, he diligently carried out the responsibilities of being the faithful spouse of the Virgin Mary and the foster father of God's only Son. No words of Joseph were recorded in the scriptures, yet his righteous actions immortalized him.

Everyone was happy for Joseph's betrothal to Mary, the young virtuous virgin from Nazareth. They had known each other for a long time and their betrothal had brought them another step closer to their marriage. Betrothal in their culture ratified an existing engagement, though the parties had no rights and duties until their marriage. Joseph was respected by everyone, not only because of his family's connection to the great king, David, but also due to his upright living. He was a just man who led a righteous life. All who came in contact with him were impressed by his fairness and sense of justice. Above all, he was a God-fearing man, who believed that his actions were expressions of his faith in God.

Joseph was aware of the many tasks to be accomplished before their marriage. He was building something special, a cradle in anticipation for their firstborn that God would bless them with in their marriage. He longed to see the beautiful smile on Mary's face when she would see the cradle and was eager to present it to her. He was engrossed in his work and thoughts, and he did not see her standing near him. For a moment he was startled and looked at her in amazement for this unusual visit. She was as if in a daze, yet she looked determined and ready for a journey. She informed him that she was going to visit her older cousin Elizabeth, who was expecting a baby in the near future. Even before he was able to ask her for the details, Mary said that she had found favor in God's sight and she herself was with child by the power of the Holy Spirit.

Upon hearing this news, Joseph must have sat down in shock, trying to make sense of the words. "My Mary, with child? It could never be, could it?" Questions were racing through his mind. She was so devout and godly. She would do nothing to bring disgrace to the family. Could it be true that she was carrying somebody else's child in her womb? With teary eyes he must have looked at the cradle he was making. He could not bear the thought of it being used by a child not fathered by him.

All these thoughts truly disturbed him and yet he knew he could never bring Mary to any kind of disgrace. He was aware of his religious traditions that did not tolerate infidelity and immorality. The punishment could even be stoning to death for an unmarried woman to be pregnant with a child. Being the kind, sensitive and righteous man that he was, Joseph found the solution – divorce her quietly as it was the only way to end the betrothal. If he formerly divorced her and left the scene by the time Mary returned from visiting Elizabeth, it would only be natural for people to conclude that he had vanished, not wanting to assume the responsibility of 'his' child growing in Mary's womb. He was willing to take that disgrace upon himself. He could not stand the thought of Mary being disgraced or punished in any way.

He must have been grief-stricken and heart-broken when he collapsed onto his bed. As always he lifted his heart to God in prayer and sought for His guidance. He must have turned and twisted on his straw mattress several times. In a dream he saw the smiling face of an angel who assured him that what Mary told him was true. God was acting on His promises and Mary was chosen to be the mother of the Savior. There was no need to doubt Mary and he could accept her to be his wife. Joseph must have awakened in bewilderment. As he tried to think things through, reality struck him, "God has chosen me to be the earthly father of His Son! Am I so worthy in God's sight that he was going to entrust His son to me?"

Resolved to be fully committed to his newly given mission, he must have moved quickly into action. He must have completed the work on the cradle with great care, and did some work on his home as well. Every detail had to be taken care of before Mary returned from visiting Elizabeth. His heart must have ached when he remembered his former thoughts of Mary's unfaithfulness. He was completely ready to respond to God's call and to care for Mary and the child.

Upon Mary's return, Joseph received her into his home. How joyful and humbled they felt for being chosen for this task! The Son of God was growing in Mary's womb! Weeks rolled into months and they were startled by the Emperor's announcement that everyone needed to be enrolled in their native towns as part of the census. It was going to be a long and painful journey to their ancestral town, Bethlehem, as Mary was getting closer to her childbirth. As always trusting in God's protection, Joseph led the journey. He must have inquired about her condition several times. He was hoping to obtain a place at the inn once they reached Bethlehem. But every inn seemed to be overflowing with people. No one seemed interested in taking in a full-term pregnant woman under their roof.

His frantic search only got them a manger, which seemed an unlikely place for the birth of the Savior. The Savior of the world, through whom everything was created, finding no place to be born! The busy town did not seem to care about what was happening in their midst. The visit of the lowly shepherds and Magi seemed to indicate that there were people who waited in anticipation for the coming of the Messiah. Mary and Joseph looked at the peaceful infant lying in the manger. He looked so fragile and helpless! When they touched Him, they knew they were touching God and when they kissed him they knew they were kissing the face of God. The whole creation around them stood still in that perfect night when heaven was wedded to earth, and God took the initiative through His Son to enter the world and to show His love.

The peaceful and joyful occasion of the birth was suddenly disturbed by another dream. The king wanted the life of the newborn. "Who on earth would want to harm a harmless baby?" Joseph must have wondered. Carefully he steadied Mary and lovingly placed her on the donkey with the baby and left for Egypt at once. Constantly he was on the lookout for the soldiers and avoided all main roads on their flight to Egypt. He wanted to protect the baby and Mary by all means.

"The greatest expression of love is often found in faithful actions" – author

MARY: Blessed Among Women

"Behold, I am the handmaid of the Lord. May it be done to me according to your word" (Lk 1:38).

Mary received the highest blessing from God as He chose her to be the mother of the Savior. No human person ever had the privilege of deciding who his or her mother would be except the person of Jesus. He was able to have this singular privilege because He was both God and man. The selection of Mary was not a random choice made by God. He chose her from the beginning and prepared her for this wondrous task. As a result she was "Full of Grace". She was Immaculate, as she was destined to carry within her the Son of God who was untouched by any traits of sin or evil. Her unconditional 'fiat' or 'yes' to the invitation of the angel to be the mother of the Savior and her surrender to God's will made her the most blessed among all women.

The great privilege accorded to Mary was also accompanied by enormous suffering. The prophetic words of Simeon, "a sword will pierce your heart" (Lk 2:35), had indicated possibilities of immeasurable pain and trials. Being faithful to God, she endured those moments of pain and in the process became the perfect model for humanity.

Though no details can be found in the Bible on Mary's childhood, one could imagine that she enjoyed great love and attention from her dedicated parents, Joachim and Ann. This saintly couple must have initiated Mary into a life of faith from a very young age. Though learning was reserved mostly for the males, Mary's parents must have taught her to read and write. What interested her the most was God's Word in the scriptures. She could read, reflect, pray and meditate on God's word for hours. The only One who could possess her completely had already claimed her even without her knowing it. The Word, that she read, reflected, prayed and meditated upon was constantly in her heart, and the Word was about to 'become flesh' in her womb in the person of Jesus!

As per the cultural practices of her time, she was betrothed at a young age with the promise of marriage in the future. She considered herself fortunate to be betrothed to Joseph, a virtuous person. She believed that God's plans were always for the good of human beings and she constantly sought the strength to do His will in her life.

She was so caught up in her thoughts that she did not immediately notice brightness all around her. Suddenly she was looking at the face of an angel who greeted her "Hail, favored one! The Lord is with you" (Lk 1:28). The message of the angel that she was chosen to be the mother of the Savior was both astonishing and unexpected. Amazed at this greatest honor, she could only ask a simple question, "How can this be since I am a virgin?" She received the reply, "The Holy Spirit will overshadow you, and the Son born will be the holy one of God" (Lk 1:34-35).

Anyone would have been ecstatic at such great news. However, Mary must have realized the enormous challenges and struggles entailed in this invitation as she was well aware of her religious and cultural practices. Pregnancy outside of marriage caused great disgrace to the family.

For the woman, punishment could be as severe as death by stoning. She was betrothed to Joseph and she knew him as a kind and just person. Yet there was no assurance of Joseph's understanding and acceptance of her situation. Despite all these future struggles, Mary totally surrendered herself to God. Her response was lovely, "Behold the handmaid of the Lord, may it be done unto me according to your word" (Lk 1:38). Even though she did not fully understand what her response entailed, she humbly, but firmly said "yes". Mary had always said "yes" to God, and constantly refrained from saying "yes" to the temptations from the evil one. She was the new Eve, and she had it in her to say "yes" to God at all times.

She had every reason to proclaim this news to everyone. The words of the Prophet Isaiah were vivid in the mind of all who expected the Messiah, "The Lord will give you this sign: the virgin shall be with child, and bear a son, and shall name him Immanuel" (Is 7:14). She could have announced to everyone that she was to be the mother of the Messiah. Knowing her devout life, most people would have believed her. What she did immediately was to be at the service of Elizabeth who needed her. The meeting of these two women must have been such a joyous moment. Both women, who experienced the awesome favor of God were thanking and praising Him for making the impossible possible. Mary's song of praise indicated for sure that she was no naïve person, who was accidentally chosen by God. It revealed the strength of her character, her unfailing trust in the Lord, and her courage to submit totally to God's will.

Upon her return she pondered over Joseph's reaction. He always seemed kind and sensitive and she knew that God would inspire Joseph to come up with the right solution. Sure enough, Joseph had already made plans to take her into his home. He wanted to be devoted to Mary and the child and intended to avoid any unwanted gossip of an illegitimate child growing in Mary's womb.

It was indeed a joyful time, waiting in expectation for the birth of the Savior. Many times Mary had to remind herself that the one who would transform the course of history and the destiny of humanity was growing in her womb. Joseph and Mary were content to set aside all their personal joys for the sake of the child, expected to be born for the redemption of the world. It was only natural to refrain from any physical intimacy on account of the Son of God growing within her. It would also be natural to dedicate themselves totally and unreservedly to the newborn even after his birth.

Though God had chosen both of them for a special mission, He had not promised that life would be easy as a result of their privileges. There were several moments in her life when she faced tremendous pains and suffering: the journey to Bethlehem, the hometown of Joseph, at the later part of her pregnancy was a painstaking one; the flight into Egypt to save the child from Herod's hunt of the newborn was more burdensome; she frantically searched for the boy Jesus when he was lost in the temple; the gravest of all was to stand at the foot of the cross and watch her son dying in agony. She must have remembered the words of Simeon several times. Her son was meant for greatness, yet she would have a sword piercing her heart. She knew that the great privilege of being the mother of the Savior entailed a heavy price. Nothing swayed her from her "Yes" to God as she trusted and believed in her loving God, and her Son, Jesus.

"We say "yes" to God not for His benefit, but ours" – author

JESUS: Fulfillment of All Promises

"Have among yourself the same attitude
That is also yours in Christ Jesus,
Who though he was in the form of God,
Did not regard equality with God
Something to be grasped.

Rather he emptied himself,
Taking the form of a slave,
Coming in human likeness,
And found human in appearance,
He humbled himself,
Becoming obedient to death,
Even death on a cross.

Because of this, God greatly exalted him
And bestowed on him the name
That at the name of Jesus
Every knee should bend,
Of those in heaven and on earth
And under the earth,
And every tongue confess that
Jesus Christ is Lord,
To the glory of God the Father."
(Phil 2:5-11)

This early Christian hymn or Christological hymn that we find in St. Paul's letter to the Philippians is rich with many levels of meaning. It can speak to us about the need to imitate Christ in humility and to aspire to the same attitudes that he exhibited in his life. It can remind us of the great self-emptying of Christ, the second person of the Trinity, who took flesh at a decisive moment in history, becoming one like us. It can tell us much more than the historical Jesus of Nazareth, who walked on this earth and died on the cross. It can remind us that the Son was with the Father at all times and by his obedience to the Father's will, he obtained redemption and salvation.

Jesus stands before us as the final fulfillment of every promise of God. By self- emptying or 'kenosis', Paul does not mean that Jesus was stripped of his divinity, but rather he took upon himself human nature as well. It is as if to say his self-emptying is not any kind of depletion, but rather by an addition of the human nature into his one person. Only this God-man (true God and true man) could restore human beings' lost friendship with God.

So far we reflected upon twenty-four persons in the Bible. We came across their many experiences, strengths, weakness, struggles and triumphs. Every one of them, in one way or the other, can teach us something about Christ. But none can take the place of His mission for humanity.

Jesus and Adam: The first Adam yielded to the temptation of evil, allowed the power of evil to intimidate and trick him. Through this act of disobedience sin and death entered the world. Jesus the New Adam resisted temptation and defeated evil by his act of obedience to the will of the Father. Through Him redemption and salvation were reclaimed.

Jesus and Eve: The first Eve's act of disobedience brought about the continuous struggle between human beings and the power of evil. Jesus, born of the new Eve, Mary, would crush the head of the serpent, the symbol of evil, and claim the decisive victory for human beings.

Jesus and Cain: Cain consumed by jealousy and anger, murdered his innocent brother Abel. Jesus, filled with compassion and love, would give up his life for sinful human beings.

Jesus and Abel: Abel's death would remind us that even an innocent person can be a victim of unexpected tragedies and raging violence. Jesus would remind his followers, "do not be afraid of those who kill the body but after that can do no more... but be afraid of the one, who, after killing, has the power to cast into Gehenna" (Lk 12:4-5).

Jesus and Noah: Noah's righteous living spared humanity from total extinction. Jesus' act of sacrifice would redeem human beings from eternal death.

Jesus and Abraham: Abraham believed, hoping against all hope and surrendered himself totally to God against all odds. "By faith Abraham, when put to the test, offered up Isaac..... He reasoned that God was able to raise even from the dead, and he received Isaac back as a symbol" (Heb 11:17-19). Jesus became the priest and sacrificial victim on the altar of the cross. There was no other creature to replace him and he surrendered totally when he said, "Father into your hands I commend my spirit".

Jesus and Esau: Esau sold his birthright for a bowl of soup. He seemed more interested in satisfying his physical needs than being part of a covenanted relationship with God. Jesus would say to the devil, "One does not live by bread alone, but by every word that comes forth from the mouth of God" (Mt 4:4).

Jesus and Jacob: Jacob exemplified perseverance and oriented his life to achieve greatness. Once he knew that it was through him God's promises would pass down to the next generation, he was determined to achieve it. Jesus would instill in his disciples that true greatness is achieved only through a life of service.

Jesus and Joseph: Joseph was sold by his own brothers to the Ishmaelites for twenty pieces of silver. Jesus would be betrayed by his chosen disciple Judas for thirty pieces of silver.

Jesus and Moses: Moses would give the Ten Commandments to the people of Israel at Mount Sinai. Jesus, the New Moses, would teach the true implications of the Commandments at his Sermon on the Mount and give the great New Commandment of Love: Love God, love your neighbor.

Jesus and Joshua: Joshua was instrumental in the conquest of the Promised Land. Jesus, through his message of love, death and resurrection, would show a new way to conquer the world, change lives and enter the eternal heavenly kingdom.

Jesus and Ruth: The humble filial piety of Ruth was blessed beyond her imagination, as she became an ancestress of the

Savior. Jesus would make it clear that every single good act is seen and rewarded by God as he lavishly praised the sacrificial offering of the poor widow at the temple (Mk 12:1-4).

Jesus and Saul: Initially Saul had everything in him to be remembered as one of the greatest kings of Israel, but as he moved away from God's ways, his life became a failure. Jesus continuously taught the disciples to abide in him to produce abundant fruits.

Jesus and David: Under David, the 12 tribes of Israel would come together as a united kingdom. The new kingdom initiated by Jesus would embrace people of every nation, language and culture. The church, built upon the foundation of twelve Apostles (symbolic of twelve tribes), would become the new home for all peoples.

Jesus and Solomon: Solomon was given the great gift of wisdom that enabled him to distinguish right from wrong. God blessed him abundantly with riches, possessions, reputation and fame. Yet Solomon in his old age turned his back on God. "Jesus advanced in wisdom and age and favor before God and human beings" (Lk 2:52). Jesus' wisdom enabled him to complete his mission as he surrendered himself totally to will of His Father.

Jesus and Jonah: Jonah did not want God to show mercy and forgiveness to the people of Nineveh. He wanted God to destroy them. Jesus says, "For God so loved the world that he gave his only Son… God did not send his Son into the world to condemn the world, but that the world might be saved through him" (Jn 3:6-17)

Jesus and Job: Job, who sought answers from the Lord for his suffering, ultimately agreed that many things in life would be unintelligible to a mere human mind: "I have dealt with great things that I do not understand; things too wonderful for me, which I cannot know" (Job 42:2). Every form of suffering and pain has a redeeming value when seen from the perspective of Calvary, where Jesus suffered and died for our sins.

Jesus and Elijah: The great prophet who was running away from the wrath of Jezebel would lay down in the desert, wishing to die. The angel ministered to him, asking him to get up and eat for the long journey ahead. Jesus would experience tremendous agony and pain in the Garden of Gethsemane. The angel ministered to him, strengthening him to face the cross and death ahead.

Jesus and Jezebel: Jezebel's belief in her false god became her ultimate enemy. Even after she was confronted with the truth, she did not want to change her evil ways. Jesus would warn the church to be very careful about the Spirit of Jezebel that could lead believers away from the truth (cf. Rev 3: 20-22).

Jesus and Jeremiah: Jeremiah announced the coming of days when God would establish a New Covenant with all the people. At the Last Supper, the day before he died, Jesus would take the cup and give it to his disciples saying, "This cup is the New Covenant in my blood, which will be shed for you" (Lk 22:20).

Jesus and Zechariah: When the angel announced to Zechariah that his prayer was heard, Zechariah would express doubt. Jesus, before raising Lazarus, would express his tremendous confidence in the Father who always listened to his prayers: "Father, I thank you for hearing. I know that you always hear" (Jn 11:41-42).

Jesus and Elizabeth: Elizabeth, in hearing Mary greet her, would exclaim with joy and acknowledge the presence of the Lord in Mary's womb: "Most blessed are you among women, and blessed is the fruit of your womb..... who am I that the mother of my Lord should come to me?" (Lk 1: 42-43). Jesus would say to Thomas, "Have you come to believe because you have seen me? Blessed are those who have not seen and yet have believed" (Jn 20:29).

Jesus and John the Baptist: John the Baptist was sent to prepare the way of the Messiah. Jesus would proclaim, "I am the way, and the truth and the life. No one comes to the Father except through me" (Jn 14:6).

Jesus and Joseph: "When Joseph awoke, he did as the angel of the Lord had commanded him and took his wife Mary into his home" (Mt 1:24). "Jesus went down with them and came to Nazareth, and was obedient to them (Mary and Joseph); and his mother kept all these things storied in her heart (Lk 1:51). We can only gasp as we think of Jesus, the second person of the Trinity, being obedient to the human authority of his parents.

Jesus and Mary: Mary surrendered to God's will when she said, "Behold the handmaid of the Lord may it be done unto me according to your word" (Lk 1:38); and she gave birth to the Savior. Jesus surrendered himself to the Father when he said, "Father, if it is possible, take this cup away from me, but not my will, but yours be done" (Lk 22:42). By these words he gave himself up to death so to give us life, life in abundance.